*Crosscurrents*/MODERN CRITIQUES

Crosscurrents/MODERN CRITIQUES

Harry T. Moore, *General Editor*

Saul Bellow's Fiction

Irving Malin

WITH A PREFACE BY
Harry T. Moore

SOUTHERN ILLINOIS UNIVERSITY PRESS
Carbondale and Edwardsville

FEFFER & SIMONS, INC.
London and Amsterdam

for my mother

The appearance of Dangling Man in 1944 marked the advent of an important new novelist. As Irving Malin says in the present book, Dangling Man echoed Dostoevsky and Kafka. At the same time, however, there was something highly original in Saul Bellow's vision of alienation, a vision which has manifested itself in his five succeeding novels.

In the first of them, the man was dangling because he was caught in the suspense of time between the moment when his draft board told him to stand by and the moment when they would call him up. But, in spite of all these familiarities and derivations, Joseph was a highly individualized and living young man. And most of Bellow's subsequent characters have also been highly individualized and living.

That is one of his great successes as a writer. But he also has control of a style that is moderately cool, intellectually resourceful, and always flexible. In addition, Bellow has something which Hemingway had in quite a different way: a compelling sense of the moods of the time. If his work is distinctively individual, it is also distinctively representative.

He is evidently a writer who takes his time, for he has produced only six novels over a span of two decades. Sometimes there have been five- or six-year intervals between the books. Bellow has filled the interim periods by accepting professorial and other academic assignments, and by writing stories and articles. In the latter he speaks with mature authority for the writer of today.

Among his novels, I care least for the two which tend toward "epic" dimensions, The Adventures of Augie March (1954) and Henderson the Rain King (1959), partly because they seem somewhat diffuse to me, lacking the concentrated intensity of The Victim (1947) and Seize the Day (1957). In caring less for Augie and Henderson I am not taking a lonely position; in the present book Irving Malin shows that he is among those commentators who hold it. Augie and Henderson are nevertheless full of fine things, including some excellent comedy. Augie March is usually spoken of as picaresque, and it is certainly in the tradition of that genre; Augie himself is very much the wandering rogue, but one who is essentially an innocent, one who is almost naïvely in quest of his identity. Henderson is quite different, far more fantastic-fabulous. The imaginary Africa is an interesting creative achievement by a man who received a university degree with honors in anthropology.

His most recent novel, Herzog (1964), is also spacious and diffuse, but it manages to compel one's attention more firmly than Augie March or Henderson. One reason may be that the Jewish Herzog is more "typical," even for non-Jewish readers, than Augie or the non-Jewish Henderson are. His very franticness has an appeal. It is profoundly representative of its time.

My own two favorites among Bellow's novels, however, remain The Victim and Seize the Day. The first of these, which really has two victims (Allbee as well as Leventhal is the victim of Allbee), is a notable dramatic diagnosis of anti-Semitism and in all ways a gripping story. The modern city, so important in The Victim, is a dominant actor in Seize the Day, with its portrait of the lost man in the upper Broadway residential hotel. These are two of the finest novels to come out of America since World War II, and they give plausibility to Irving Malin's opening sentence, which by hedging a bit avoids being flatly dogmatic: "Saul Bellow is probably the most important living American novelist."

Mr. Malin's detailed study of Bellow's work attempts to show why this might be. It is a highly sympathetic critical exposition, particularly in its investigations of Bellow's themes and characters. At the present stage of Saul Bellow's career, this is a valuable, even a necessary book.

HARRY T. MOORE

Southern Illinois University
August 16, 1968

Contents

Introduction

Saul Bellow is probably the most important living American novelist. Although he has not yet reached the limits of his talent, he has already produced six novels which deserve close study.

This book is arranged simply. In the first chapter I explore the world of Bellow as it appears in "Two Morning Monologues," his first published story. Then I discuss five themes—*moha*, madness, time, masquerade, and Jewishness—which seem to be his basic ideas. In the third chapter I limit my discussion to his characters. In the next two chapters I chart those images and styles which express or incarnate theme and character. And my final chapter, before the brief conclusion, is devoted to *Herzog* which exemplifies impressively his fictional achievement.

From the following chapters the reader can see that I am biased—I omit biography (using Bellow's non-fiction as my only "biographical" references); I limit my discussion of his relatively weak stories; I am "vertical" rather than "horizontal." But I hope that my approach is, despite these omissions or limitations, a valid one to Bellow's fictional kingdom.

I wish to thank the Corporation of Yaddo for a residence fellowship in the summer of 1963. I also thank Saul Bellow, A. M. Heath & Company, Ltd., The Viking Press, and Weidenfeld & Nicolson, Ltd., for permission to use extracts from *Seize the Day, Henderson the Rain King, Herzog*, and *The Adven-*

tures of Augie March. Quotations from "Dangling Man" are reprinted by permission of Laurence Pollinger, Ltd., Weidenfeld and Nicolson, Ltd., and the publishers, The Vanguard Press, from "Dangling Man" by Saul Bellow. Copyright, 1944, by the Vanguard Press, Inc.; quotations from "The Victim" are also reprinted by permission of the publishers, The Vanguard Press, from "The Victim" by Saul Bellow. Copyright, 1947, by Saul Bellow. And I thank *Partisan Review* for permission to quote from "Two Morning Monologues" © 1941 by *Partisan Review*.

Portions of this book have appeared in *Jewish Heritage, London Magazine,* my *Jews and Americans* (Southern Illinois University Press, 1965), and my *Saul Bellow and the Critics* (New York University Press, 1967). I wish to thank the Commission on Adult Jewish Education for the use of my article, "The Jewishness of Saul Bellow," reprinted with permission from *Jewish Heritage* (Summer, 1964), a publication of B'nai B'rith's Commission on Adult Jewish Education; thanks also to New York University Press for permission to reprint "Seven Images" © 1967 by New York University; and I wish to thank the editors of *London Magazine* for permission to reprint my article, "Saul Bellow," which appeared in January, 1965.

IRVING MALIN

City College of New York
March 18, 1968

Saul Bellow's Fiction

1

The First Story

Perhaps the best introduction to Bellow's world—to its themes, characters, and images—is his first piece of fiction, "Two Morning Monologues," which appeared in the May–June, 1941 issue of *Partisan Review*.

Mandelbaum, the first speaker, tells us how he spends his day "without work." He disposes of this day —and, we assume, every day—by fruitlessly looking for a job, "pulling the marrow out of a cigarette," taking an "extravagant boat ride," or reading in the library. The second speaker muses about the "angles" of the day's race, the first cigarette, and breakfast. These men are less concerned with physical action than meditation and conversation.

What characteristic themes are stated? Mandelbaum and the gambler live in a completely alien society. In the opening paragraph we read that Mandelbaum, the unemployed son, is "driven": he cannot stay at home because he refuses to accept the compelling, self-centered designs of his parents, especially those of his father. He does not want to work just to earn money and please everybody. He wants more than the "fat gods." [1] The gambler, on the other hand, goes along with the system, but even he thinks it's a "sour loss"—the workaday routine is meaningless because it doesn't satisfy his soul: "The sucker scraping the griddle, turning the eggs, paddling the bread with wet butter. I couldn't put in his twelve hours."

Must such alert men accept the patterns of society?

Must they be mere worshippers of fact and figures? Must they love money? Mandelbaum thinks: "Total it any way, top to bottom, reverse the order, it makes no difference, the sum is always *sunk*." The gambler agrees with him: "To get around it counts. Slipping through." They both rebel against the fundamentally destructive system; at the same time they find that they have no values of their own. Thus they feel guilty or depressed. Although "Two Morning Monologues" stresses the "literal" social fact, it is almost "metaphysical." The system is, after all, the world we know—the world we did not make but adopted. The speakers are concerned with more than functions of money; they want to *know themselves in relation to universals*—the gambler asks: "Who picks us out?" The world itself is presented as the necessary, inescapable design which challenges individual identity: "Here we are. What'll it be today, the library? museum? the courthouse? a convention?"

Bellow emphasizes painful irresolution: rebellion versus submission; narcissism versus communion; and fear versus courage. Because the speakers are torn by such "double" values, they are, in the end, on the "edge of being." The gambler knows that even this edge may be an illusion, another appearance which hides reality. He counsels himself: "Walk on the edge without falling." At the same time he knows that he *can* fall. He wants, at times, to close his eyes. So does Mandelbaum: "Eventually it will be settled, but the space between eventually and the present is long enough to stretch my legs in."

Bellow suggests that "time is of the essence." This day must be confronted, understood, and mastered. The speakers have to seize it, knowing that it carries the burdens of past and future. Again there is ambivalence: this day resembles other days, but it is unique. How can they live in the *system* of time? How can they be *in* and *out* of history? I take these questions to be crucial in both monologues. Mandelbaum knows that his father bought the house—the symbolic burden —long ago. The gambler also thinks of the past he carries—not of his father's house but of his childhood: "When you come to it there's a lot that has to do with what remains of it from childhood." Gambling is a fitting symbol of time's ways: we are handed cards; we must act now; but we don't know what cards we will choose.

Bellow gives us family relationships as he does in his novels. Mandelbaum's father is not a "monster," but he does seem to be full of self-love. When he says that his son is a "good boy, a smart boy," he demonstrates that he is proud of him, yet he also feels that he is better than this smart boy: *he*, after all, is working. The father creates an atmosphere of competition; he proclaims by all of his deeds—by advertising for a job, by making him feel "wrong and guilty," by mentioning the other smart boys—that he commands his son.

Mandelbaum gets little help from his mother. Although she is "much gentler" than the father, she is clumsy in her affection,

> Ordinarily she is as strange to me as though she were dead or nonexistent. But then, when I recognize that she is alive—not only that she lives, but that she prepares my orange juice before I leave and hands me my lunch—it gives me an extraordinary twist. I am the only son.

The mother offers orange juice—little else. It is characteristic that Bellow's speaker regards her with more love than he does his father—at least she won't scold him! But I think she is as "dangerous" as her husband. The family ties—muted though they are—suggest that Mandelbaum learns to dangle at home.

And his view of the "outside" world is corrupted. He knows that society resembles—or projects—his father's absurd conceptions, and he reacts toward the people he encounters, especially prospective employers, in the same immature way. He is a son unsure of his identity; he is treated as such by those who have "purpose and money and influence."

The gambler also regards society as a "conventional" parent, but unlike his alter ego, he reacts as a "mean" boy. He is a hostile name-caller: the others are "fall guys," "suckers," enemies. It is interesting that he is superstitious:

> When you come to it there's a lot that has to do with what remains of it from childhood. . . . Kids think they can control the world. Walk from one side of the room to the other and a bell will ring; throw a stone at the sky and wait for it to rain. Next time it will rain. I remember that.

The gambler, like "uncivilized" natives, is awed by worldly tricks. He sees many mysterious strangers.

Both speakers are more concerned with their conflicts, with ideas of power, than with sex. We don't see much of Mandelbaum's mind, but it is safe to say that he finds no comfort with women, who, perhaps, mirror his gentle, "dead" mother; he knows that they don't count—they can't help him assert his strength. He is a bachelor. The gambler, similarly, doesn't mention girls—not even Lady Luck. They are not important in his "will to power" because he probably thinks of them as conventional or honest. Men he can "fight back with a stick."

There are several images in "Two Morning Monologues" which recur in the novels: "rooms," voyages, and "mirrors." Bellow does not go far; he does not create exotic images to represent the plight of his heroes. The "room" is the prison of spirit. Mandelbaum continually finds himself *confined*: the "stairs have become darker, more buckled and gap-jointed"; he waits at the agency, "sitting on benches, crossing and recrossing [his] legs with the others, reading the signs forbidding smoking and stating the rates of the agency"; he thinks of the "closely curled leaves" of his identity; he hopes to strike "the secret panel of the sliding door." The gambler wants to "get around it"; he wants to open the door, to "slip through." He also is "squeezed" by the condition in which he finds himself.

Bellow opposes movement to confinement. But the movement is erratic, violent, or non-purposeful. The unemployed son is "driven" from the house. He takes a "long ride," paying "little attention" to the sights. He likes to "lounge several hours in one place," rather than take an "extravagant boat ride." The gambler's motion is more violent: the cigarette "dizzies" him; he wants to go "through the cracks"; he thinks of planes "colliding in all the room in the world," of skyscrapers toppling, of cards falling. He hears, finally, the "swishing in the heart like a deck riffled."

Bellow also uses often-inverted reflections to express the ambiguities of life. He characteristically gives us *two* monologues, juxtaposing the docility of Mandelbaum to the anger of the gambler. Indeed, these heroes—"good boy" and gambler, lounger and racer, innocent and con-man—prefigure the doubles in all of his novels. Nor does he neglect other kinds of reflection. Consider Mandelbaum thinking of Bobby Poland, the neighbor's son, who is the same age. This "brother" is an accountant. Earlier he sees himself in those who are out of work, but his father thinks that he is "different." The gambler refers to contrasts, inversions, reflections: "You have to be able to recognize them." He recognizes that he is unlike the fall guys; he is disturbed by those who don't look and step where they "shouldn't"; he glances at the eyes of the other players. But his vision of reality is as clouded as the mirror touched by his cigarette smoke.

The style of "Two Morning Monologues" prefigures later developments. Mandelbaum and the gambler speak. Immediately we feel that they are communicating directly to us; no "author" interrupts their monologues. Bellow suggests that "style is the man," that fiction embodies personal truth. We respond to sincerely expressed troubles. Listen to Mandelbaum: "It's my father's fault that I'm driven from the house all morning and most of the afternoon. I'm supposed to be looking for a job. I don't exaggerate when I say driven. That's what it is." He speaks urgently, simply, often uncontrollably. Rarely does he use imagery: "This morning [the descending sun] makes me think of nothing more important than a paper seal on a breakfast food box. Yank it and the box opens. You will find a toy prize on top; a toy plane, crossed snowshoes, a tiny loving cup." This typical image expresses his "practical," down-to-earth view of nature, his concern with food and prizes which await him. When Mandelbaum becomes poetic, he still remains close to home: he mentions the "closely curled leaves" of identity, but he juxtaposes this image to the sandwich he carries in his pocket. Bellow mediates between the literal and the symbolic, understanding that this linkage is often amusing. Consequently, Mandelbaum refers to finding "unusual resources"—learning to "suck a maximum from each straw and pull the marrow out of a cigarette."

The gambler speaks distinctively:

> What does it amount to? Close my eyes and pick, I may as well. It turns out the same; mostly sour loss. System is nothing and to try to dope them is just wasted. It isn't a matter you reach into yourself for, bringing it up and showing it to the eyes, open proof. The card is dark, always, the dice to the last roll.

His monologue is rapid, sincere, and practical, but it is more "poetic" than Mandelbaum's—almost visionary: "That's it, you see, the verge, the edge, the crumb of a minute before when any one of twelve, fifty, eight, thirty-seven comes out." The vision, however, is full of "crumbs." Again Bellow is able to show the doom of "money owing, rent postponed, hole in your glove, one egg, cheap tobacco." His lists convey the puzzling density of life.

2

The Themes

Bellow views contemporary society as a threat. Everywhere there are things—goods, appliances, and false information—which "distract" us:

> The shops are filled with goods and buyers. In the fields were the newest harvesting machines; in the houses washers, dryers, freezers and refrigerators, air conditioners, vacuum cleaners, Mixmasters, Waringblenders, television and stereophonic high-fi sets, electrical can openers, novels condensed by the *Reader's Digest* and slick magazines. In the yards, glossy cars in giddy colors, like ships from outer space.[1]

Because we are surrounded by such attractive things, we don't realize that they can be destructive. The "reign of the fat gods"[2] is not simply dull: "It destroys and consumes everything, it covers the human image with deadly films, it undermines all quality with its secret rage, it subverts everything good and exalts lies, and on its rotten head it wears a crown of normalcy."[3] Bellow believes that our "Pig Heaven"[4] contaminates human dignity—we no longer have a sense of uniqueness. We become another "commodity," relinquishing not only our ability to rebel against the system but our insight. We misrepresent ourselves: we assume "false greatness" if we accept the values and gain success; we assume "false insignificance" if we don't accept the values and find failure.[5] "On either side we have the black and white of paranoia." [6] There is really no free choice—we yield to social drives.

The terrifying *density* of society is always suggested in Bellow's novels. In *Dangling Man* Joseph muses:

> I . . . settle down to read the paper in the rocker by the window. I cover it from end to end, ritualistically, missing not a word. First come the comic strips . . . , then I read the serious news and the columnists, and finally the gossip, the family page, the recipes, the obituaries, the society news, the ads, the children's puzzles, everything.

The newspaper—with its crowded, paralyzing columns —perfectly reflects the "sameness" of everything: recipes, puzzles, serious news, and gossip are equally valuable or important. Erich Fromm puts the matter of lost distinctions this way: "Newspapers tell us the trite thoughts or breakfast habits of a debutante with the same space and seriousness they use for reporting events of scientific or artistic importance." [7] He also realizes that this condition is not to be laughed at: We are no longer able to think critically; "eventually our attitude to what is going on in the world assumes a quality of flatness and indifference." [8]

Not only does Bellow use the newspaper list—he constantly offers lists of food, furniture, and clothing to create the "thinginess" we encounter daily. Here is food in *The Adventures of Augie March*:

> The meals were of amazing character and of huge quantity—Anna was a strong believer in eating. Bowls of macaroni without salt or pepper or butter or sauce, brain stews and lung stews, calves'-foot jelly with bits of calves' hair and sliced egg, cold pickled fish, crumb-stuffed tripes, canned clam chowder, and big bottles of orange pop.

Again there are no qualifications—only *food*.

Bellow, of course, knows that our society has more luxuries than past societies, but he sees an "eternal" opposition of *moha* to the spirit. In *The Adventures of Augie March* Kayo explains that these finite things which "overshadow" us—meat on the table, newspaper columns, heat in our pipes—are "all external and the same." The only redemption from *moha* is love. But we cannot redeem ourselves or escape from *moha* because we ourselves are transformed.

Look, for example, at *Dangling Man.* Joseph rereads the lists and stares so much at solitary objects in his closed room that he finally studies himself as a thing. Even he has more humanity than his friend, Morris, who hypnotizes Minna and uses her for a malicious experiment—she becomes "less specifically . . . a woman than a more generalized human being—and a sad one, at that." Later Joseph pictures the body in a grotesque way: "There was a Parisian cripple in the days of John Law, the Scottish speculator, who stood in the streets renting out his hump for a writing desk to people who had no convenient place to take their transactions." The Farsons, Joseph's friends, disregard their baby's humanity—they send her to their parents, while they themselves go to California.

The metaphysical concern with *moha* is apparent in *The Victim.* Leventhal meditates:

> Man is weak and breakable, has to have just the right amounts of everything—water, air, food; can't eat twigs and stones; has to keep his bones from breaking and his fat from melting. This and that. Hoards sugar and potatoes, hides money in his mattress.

He regards the body as an egg; life becomes an "egg race." It is easy to succumb to such a distracted, materialistic view of oneself. Augie March realizes that even art objects in the past were "dangerous"; however, they were still related to but *different* from humanity. Now "it's the things themselves, the products that are distinguished, and the individual man isn't equal to their great sum." And Henderson, as Marcus Klein indicates, "abandons things and people to make the trip to Africa." [9] Although the future rain king

rages against "junk," he continues to think in meta-
phors of things—"nameless, faceless," non-spiritual.[10]

Of course, Mr. Klein is right in asserting that the
things are equated with city life: "in the city there is
much more to contend with. Things and others both
are close and thick in Bellow's novels." [11] The one
thing—merely a scrap of green paper—which acquires
ultimate significance is the dollar. If we look "inno-
cently" at the meaning of money, we can see that it is
absurd for us to want such uninteresting paper—paper
without beauty and *quality*. We don't have to go as
far here as does Norman O. Brown in his brilliant
psychoanalytical explanation—"Filthy Lucre" in *Life
Against Death*— to claim that money is "excre-
mental." [12] Some of his comments, however, demonstrate the "truth" of Bellow's concerns: money,
things in general, "cover the human image with
deadly films." [13] Or as Brown puts it, "possessive mas-
tery over nature and vigorously economical thinking
are partial impulses in the human being (the human
body) which in modern civilization have become tyrant organizers of the whole human life." [14]

In his essays Bellow is fascinated by the problem of
money. He writes an early "Spanish Letter":

> For middle-class families without *enchufes*, the diffi-
> culties are terrible. One must wear a European suit, a
> shirt that costs two hundred pesetas, a tie. . . . One
> must cling to one's class. The fall into the one below is
> measureless. Its wretchedness is an ancient fact, stable,
> immemorial, and understood by everyone. The newer
> wretchedness, that of keeping one meager suit present-
> able, of making a place in the budget for movies in
> order to have something to contribute to polite conver-
> sation when *The Song of Bernadette* is discussed, of
> persisting to exhaustion among the stragglers in the
> chase after desirable things, the casual American, is
> nevertheless not *the* wretchedness. That you see in the
> tenements and the inhabited ruins, old kilns and caves,
> the human swarms in the dry rot of Vallecas and
> Mataderos.[15]

But "*the* wretchedness" is a first step toward self-knowledge. Poverty at least forces human beings to return from *moha* to their own real image:

> Human history can fairly be described upon one level as the history of scarcity, and now that technology extends the promise of an increase of wealth we had better be aware of a poverty of the soul as terrible as that of the body. The lives of the poor move us, awaken compassion, but improvement of their lot merely by the increase of goods and comforts deprives them of *the sense of reality based upon their experience of scarcity*.[16] (my italics)

Poverty equals reality. How simple an explanation!

Now we can see the importance of money for Bellow's fiction. In *Dangling Man*, Joseph, and Iva, his wife, find it difficult to endure poverty—especially because *he* does not work. But, ironically enough, Joseph is thrown back on himself, learning that money is merely a thing, not so valuable as his feelings. He is different from Mr. Frink, the banker, who looks upon the poor as children or idiots. When Joseph tries to cash a check, he discovers that because he is out of work, he doesn't exist for Mr. Frink. The entire incident is "foolish"—to use his word—but so is the assumption that a piece of paper gives another person the right to regard him as a "suspicious character."

This scene resembles one meaning of Asa's plight in *The Victim*. He is persecuted by Allbee, who insists that he lost his job as a result of Asa's blustery, non-businesslike replies to Rudiger. Allbee hounds him; he wants him, at one point, to find him another job. In this "suspicious" situation the poor Allbee again demonstrates occult knowledge; the well-fed Asa doesn't know how to cope with threatening reality.

Augie March, raised in a poor home, is very conscious of the falseness of money; at the same time he desperately needs it. Perhaps the following remarks indicate his unwilling attraction to it.

I saw anew how great a subject money is in itself. Here was vast humankind that meshed or dug, or carried, picked up, held, that served, returning every day to its occupations, and being honest or kidding or weeping or hypocritic or mesmeric, and money, if not the secret, was anyhow beside the secret, as the secret's relative, or associate or representative before the peoples.

In *Seize the Day* Tommy Wilhelm finds himself in debt to his wife (alimony payments), and the hotel (rent).[17] He gives his last savings to Dr. Tamkin, a charlatan psychologist, for investment in stocks. "Tamkin's Folly," he hears his father say, and the phrase captures him, for as he admits, "When it comes to women and money, I'm completely in the dark." But the very fact that he fails to understand the "money-flow" makes him close to reality. He is not so aggressive or "insane" as the psychologist, who says (with unsuspecting irony?): "Money-making is aggressive. That's the whole thing. . . People come to the market to kill . . . Only they haven't got the genuine courage to kill, and they erect a symbol of it. The money. They make a killing by a fantasy." Tommy understands the system's madness.

So does Clarence Feiler in "The Gonzaga Manuscripts." Like the "childish" Tommy he believes in poetry, spirit, and ideals, but he discovers that the money-flow has corrupted European traditions and disfigured poetry. When he attempts to locate the Gonzaga manuscripts, he finds that the Spanish relatives and friends of the dead poet consider poetry as "worthless" and Clarence's quest as a con-game. They act accordingly:

> "Is this—It can't be. You've given me the wrong thing." His heart was racing. Look in your pocket again."
> "The wrong thing?"
> "It looks like shares of stock."
> "Then it isn't the wrong thing. It's what it's supposed

to be; mining stock. Isn't that what you're interested in?"

"Of course not! Certainly not!"

The husband in "The Wrecker" (a one-act play) doesn't value money. He refuses to accept the bonus given to him by the city, which intends to build on his property. He believes, in fact, that he should be allowed to destroy his own home—without pay. The city employee merely regards him as a lunatic or criminal. Henderson, the rain king also refuses to accept money. Although he is worth "three million dollars" after taxes, he becomes a "bum." He regards his wealth as an unnecessary burden from which he must escape. He travels to Africa, where the dollar is less meaningful than cows or lions. There it is, once more, only paper, lacking natural mystery.

Bellow stresses the "madness" of contemporary society. In "The Sealed Treasure" he writes: "On either side we have the black and white of paranoia." [18] "Disorder and disharmony" are discussed in "Distractions of a Fiction Writer." [19] What exactly is the madness? How does it arise? The key components are *narcissism, abstractionism,* and *compulsion.* Because our society "does not do much to help the American come of age," it "provides no effective form." [20] We are always thrown back upon ourselves to establish the form to fight *moha.* But we are so anxious, that we become self-absorbed, afraid to leave our "deaf, . . . mutilated and peculiarly ignorant" self.[21] Gradually we begin to love our form, despite the fact that it is "cracked." Narcissism arises from impotence. Or as Fromm writes: "economic conditions . . . [make] for increasing isolation and powerlessness." [22]

The powerlessness (loved and hated) can force two reactions:

this powerlessness leads either to the kind of escape that we find in the authoritarian character, or else to a

compulsive conforming in the process of which the
isolated individual becomes an automaton, loses his
self, and yet at the same time consciously conceives of
himself as free and subject only to himself.[23]

Because we regard ourselves as "giddy cars," we become nonhuman and "automatic." We consider others as objects or stereotypes to be manipulated so that
we can assert the power we lack. Mr. Frink, in the
scene from *Dangling Man*, loves his position of power,
but at the same time, feels threatened: he treats Joseph as a name, not as a human being. The weak
narcissist must always regard others as abstractions; he
cannot accept them as being as important as himself
—such acceptance could shatter his self-image. Thus
compulsion enters. The narcissist is caught in a never-
ending process. He can no longer choose freely—any
choice which is made is likely to be absurd, grandiose,
childish.

Although Bellow does not give us this *analytic* picture, he is very aware of narcissism, abstractionism,
and compulsion. Here are typical statements from his
essays and reviews. In "Distractions of a Fiction
Writer," he says that "the writer has no connection
with power, and yet he keeps thinking about it." [24] He
goes on to discuss impotence as a characteristic theme
of modern literature, finding it in such works as *Moby
Dick*, "The Beast in the Jungle," *Oblomov*, and *Ulysses*. It is clear that Ahab, John Marcher, Oblomov,
and Leopold Bloom are all "mad." Marcher, for example, waits for the Beast to spring out at him, but this
waiting becomes compulsive—so much so that he falls
in love with It and cannot love May Bartram. The
same kind of relationship destroys Captain Ahab. In
an article on Dostoyevsky, Bellow distrusts the self-
centeredness of the French (and of the Russian writer's characters).[25] Reviewing Philip Young's book on
Hemingway, he elaborates on the "self-absorption" of
Hemingway and his attempt to come to terms with it:
Hemingway shows in his fiction a "need for liberation

from dominance of the mind," a need, that is, to break out of his self-imposed circle of abstractionism.[26]

Other critics have noted madness in Bellow's fiction, but they have not defined it in terms of the three components. Herbert Gold has written: "All of Saul Bellow's novels have contained intensely personal visions of desire at the dark limits of the soul where desire becomes obsession."[27] Dan Jacobson echoes this: "It is worth noting that in all the books the consciousness of the hero is the consciousness of the book."[28] This consciousness is often obsessive. Mr. Jacobson continues: "if we are to go back into American literature to find parallels for one of the strongest elements in Mr. Bellow's work there are darker figures . . . to be named. Ahab and Bartleby the Scrivener are solitaries too, even monomaniacs."[29] Edmund Bergler writes about the masochism in *The Adventures of Augie March*: "The missing link consists of frantic avoidance of the most decisive human motivation: unconscious masochism.[30] He complains that Bellow doesn't explain why Augie is an "unconscious seeker of the pleasure—in displeasure pattern."[31] Leslie Fiedler refers to the "hysteria and catalepsy" of Bellow's style.[32]

In *Dangling Man* Joseph notes the compulsive way people assert toughness or—as he calls it—"harboiled-dom." Because of this "code," they inhibit "serious" feelings. He does not want to succumb to this madness, but the very fact that he keeps a journal means that he is probably as compulsive as the others. He also adopts a rigid pattern which soothes his troubled spirit; he resembles Oblomov, rarely leaving his room.

Bellow extends the range of madness. The Army regards Joseph as an abstraction—3A or 1A—not as an individual. The maid smokes as she cleans his room because she views him objectively. Mr. Vanaker, the "werewolf" neighbor, proclaims his power by slamming doors, "snooping through the house," and viewing the other roomers with contempt. When Joseph visits his in-laws, he finds the same mad reactions. Mr. Almstadt has submitted to the self-centered designs of his wife, who shrewishly commands him (and Joseph). Joseph thinks that all these people—relatives or strangers—have lost their sanity. *Moha* and madness are inextricably bound:

> There must be a difference, a quality that eluded me, somehow, a difference between things and persons and even between acts and persons. Otherwise the people who lived here were actually a reflection of the things they lived among. I had always striven to avoid blaming them. Was that not in effect behind my daily reading of the paper? In their businesses and politics, their taverns, movies, I tried continually to find clear signs of their common humanity.

Ironically enough, he regards the others as "common humanity," but this consideration is slightly dangerous because the *others become an abstraction.* Joseph wants desperately to see himself in them; he wants them, moreover, to mirror his plight. Most critics see Joseph as a "lover," but I wonder how an "unwilling" narcissist can trust others enough to accept individual differences. It is very easy to love humanity, groups, organizations, more difficult to love individuals. At least Joseph is human because he is ambivalent; the people he meets are not because they refuse to acknowledge "split" attitudes. And he does not hurt anyone—except himself.

The party Joseph and Iva go to becomes a ritual of inhuman madness; someone says: "*they* come when everybody's high so that they can stand around and watch us make fools of themselves." People are "grouped together indistinctly." Robbie Stillman "was under a compulsion to finish [a joke] no one wanted to hear finished . . ."—a joke repeated "any number of times." Morris Abt "objectifies" Minna. *This hypnosis emerges as the "objective correlative" of all the preceding madness.* The girl is treated as a thing to be manipulated; by asserting his power, Morris loves himself a bit more.

Dangling Man also contains the "ideal construction." Joseph thinks that we are anxious creatures who establish a "form" by which we live—the form is usually "insane" because we find no proper, flexible patterns around us. The ideal construction is restrictive; other people must fit into it. Bellow has already given us characters—Morris, the maid, Myron—who live with unconscious, half-formed constructions. Joseph, however, is extremely aware of his own. Looking back at his "older self" of a year ago, he says: "He does not have what people call an 'open' look, but is restrained—at times, despite his amiability, forbidding. He is a person greatly concerned with keeping intact." Joseph plays roles, working "everything out in accordance with a general plan." He adopts friends if they *fit*. But the plan—because it is so rigid—inhibits "strangeness in the world." It strangles curiosity.

Joseph shapes his idea into a universal principle. Reasoning with himself, he says:

> An ideal construction, an obsessive device. There have been innumerable varieties: for study, for wisdom, bravery, war, the benefits of cruelty, for art; the God-man of the ancient cultures, the ecclesiastic, the despot, the ascetic, the millionaire, the manager. I could name hundreds of these ideal constructions, each with its assertions and symbols, each finding—in conduct, in God, in art, in money—its particular answer and each proclaiming: 'This is the only possible way to meet chaos.'

The ideal construction often "exhausts the man. It can become his enemy. It often does."

Now Bellow is not merely interested in Joseph's rationalization—he also believes in this universal principle, as is clear from the essays I have already mentioned. Morse Peckham, author of *Beyond the Tragic Vision*, agrees with him: cultural history, religion—all orientations—are rooted in our desire to subject chaos into ideal constructions, but these constructions often disregard reality:

> Since man cannot deal with his environment unless he experiences sufficient internal equilibrium to observe what goes on around him, one drive is toward perfect orientation; but if he devotes himself too wholeheartedly to orientative activity, he will neglect the genuinely threatening aspects of the external world.[33]

The characters in *Dangling Man* have submitted to "perfect orientation," thereby neglecting their own "threatening aspects." They have, in effect, killed themselves; they have failed to admit a "continuous restructuring of orientations." [34]

We have to live in ordered ways, but we must be flexible. Joseph quotes from Goethe: "All comfort in life is based upon a regular occurrence of external phenomena. The changes of the day and night, of the seasons, of flowers and fruits and all other recurring pleasure that come to us . . . —these are the mainsprings of our earthy life." But this very regularity becomes dull; it is viewed as "inflexible." Goethe reminds his reader of the Englishman who hanged himself so that he might no longer have to dress and undress himself every day. Joseph cannot resolve his ambivalence. At the end of the novel he accepts another ideal construction, the "regimentation" of the Army.

We find madness in *The Victim*. Even before we meet Allbee and his ideal construction, we see narcissism, compulsion, and abstractionism in isolated incidents. Mr. Beard says that Asa "takes unfair advantage like the rest of his brethren." This cold, inhibiting abstractionism opposes the "distraction or even madness" of Elena's chaotic movements. (Asa likens his sister-in-law to his mother, who had died in an insane asylum when he was eight and his brother six.) Later he is disturbed by the bell. He dreams of mice darting along the walls. He feels threatened, "unwell," perhaps because he believes he carries seeds of madness.

Allbee enters. Immediately we see that he treats Asa as an *object of play*; he knows about his wife's trip and his departure from work earlier in the day. He believes that *Asa as Jew is evil; he is to blame for everything wrong in the world.* To fight chaos he accepts this paranoid view; it enhances his self-image by giving him "secret" knowledge. Of course, Bellow does not give us a black and white picture. Asa is equally prepared to consider Allbee as evil—an evil *Gentile.* He sees the other's constant play as "some freakish, insane process." It's the only way he can keep himself intact —at all powerful. The two constructors oppose each other.

Schlossberg is one of the few sane people in New York. Unlike the others—Allbee, Asa, Rudiger—he understands that ideal constructions, cruel abstractionism, and self-centered values rob men of their humanity. Schlossberg begins his discussion by remarking that a certain actress is not human—merely "lame." She does not show in her face "fear, hate, a hard heart, cruelness, fascination." She is mechanical—so much so that "she is not a woman." Her actions parallel the mad actions of the main characters. Then Schlossberg generalizes: "Everything comes in packages. If it's in a package, you can bring the devil in the house." Humanity itself has become a commodity, something wrapped up, not allowed to flourish. Madness takes away our potentialities. There is brutal irony: Asa and Allbee are "less than human" because they have tried —especially Allbee—to be "more than human," to be godlike in their constructions. Schlossberg returns to his opening remarks: "Good acting is what is exactly human."

The Adventures of Augie March also presents madness. On the very first page we see that Grandma Lausch governs Augie, Simon, Georgie, and Mama, informing them that they must act craftily at the Charities office. Although Grandma proclaims that she is merely helping them—"You see how it is—do I have to say more? There's no man in the house and children to bring up."—she is taking away their ability to choose, their risk-filled humanity. Miraculously Augie remains "larky and boisterous." But he finds other "mad crusaders." Anna Coblin says: "I'll treat you like my own boy . . . , my own Howard." "Love" again comes into focus, but Anna's love regards Augie as an abstraction—a substitute-son. After all, anyone would do. Einhorn, like the two mothers, adopts Augie: he had a "teaching turn similar to Grandma Lausch's, both believing they could show what could be done with the world, where it gave or resisted, where you could be confident." Later Mrs. Renling too has a "mission," seeing that "there was something adoptional" about Augie—she offers him new clothing.

Bellow takes a *new view of madness*. He looks at it with humor. Here are two related examples. Einhorn decides that he will teach Augie about women; he takes him to a cat-house. The humor arises from the fact that crippled Einhorn has to be *carried* by Augie; teacher and student, "constructor" and "thing," play reverse roles. Bellow implies by this upside-down view that the "strong" lovers are slaves of compulsive narcissism. Thus the description of Mrs. Renling's mission:

> But all the same I was not going to build into Mrs. Renling's world, to consolidate what she affirmed she was. And it isn't only she but a class of people who trust they will be justified, that their thoughts will be as substantial as the seven hills to build on, and by spreading their power they will have an eternal city for vindication on the day when other founders have gone, bricks and planks, whose thoughts were not real and who built on soft swamp.

Mrs. Renling is an "eternal" builder. The juxtaposition of her silliness and Roman greatness—of two different constructions—makes Augie laugh. Of course,

Mrs. Renling is not so "paranoid" as Allbee, but her madness reflects the madness of the entire system.

And Augie himself is tinged by it. Although he wants to rest in his "own specific gravity," sitting in his "own nature"—"free even of [his] own habits"—he begins to form ideal constructions. He tells Clem that he will get a piece of property, settle down on it, set up a home, and teach school. He doesn't want the "Happy Isles," he says, but we should not accept his calm statements. Now Augie does want to build something "eternal"—after rebelling against other patterns, he wants to impose his own upon others—upon children. Clem sees through the project: "You'll give them their chance in life and rescue them, so you'll be their saint and holy father." He adds: "You do too want to be a king." Defending himself by screaming that Clem searches for "bad motives," Augie can't face his own madness. Afterwards he does. He views his "foster-home and academy dream" more realistically as a "featherhead millenarian notion."

It is surprising that most critics mention Augie's lack of commitments, without underlining the tension he has between remaining free and building ideal constructions. Robert Gorham Davis discusses his "involvement and detachment" but neglects the foster-home dream—an *involvement* of self.[35] Robert Penn Warren explains that Augie is the "man with no commitments." [36] This kind of remark is "easy," robbing Bellow of irony. Not only does he present the ideal academy—he shows us that Augie is "obsessively" aware of freedom. This "faithfulness to his image of himself as free"—to quote Chester Eisinger—becomes ideal, abstract, and compulsive.[37] When Augie talks at great length about freedom, he reminds us of Isabel Archer, who proclaims her independence but marries Gilbert Osmond. But Bellow somehow seems less detached than James. He favors Augie's ideal, without completely noting its inadequacies. Surely there is truth in Bergler's remarks about the novel: Bellow does avoid explaining the reason for obsessive involvement with no commitments.[38] Augie remains a curious, shadowy figure who runs away from himself and us.

There is madness in *Seize the Day*. Dr. Tamkin maintains that he *knows* how to beat the system—his investment scheme (which he compels Tommy to join) is based on the fact that he has more sense than other investors. He is a complete narcissist, who regards poor Tommy as a kind of sport. Again Bellow is ironic. This mad crusader is "calm and rational," but he loses this rationality because he constantly thinks of it—it becomes something over which he has no control. His first words to Tommy are: "You have a very obsessional look on your face." His statement is true—at least *we* know it applies to almost all of Bellow's characters—but it is true *only* because Tamkin always sees "obsessional looks"—except on *his* face. He thinks: "every public figure had a character-neurosis. Maddest of all were the businessmen, the heartless, flaunting, boisterous business class who ruled this country with their hard manners and their bold lies and their absurd words that nobody could believe." The doctor regards the world as a patient, projecting his own illness. His designs, theories, and games help to make Tamkin feel important. At the same time they take away his power and freedom. When he speaks about the world, we should listen carefully. Regard this statement: "all suicide is murder, and all murder is suicide." Most critics have discussed his murder of Tommy, but they have not seen his suicidal constructions.

Of course, there is some truth in Tamkin's remarks. Dr. Adler, Tommy's father, is also imprisoned in his own designs. He believes that money or "style" means more than love. Because his son is a failure, he cannot accept him—in fact, he rejects him at every turn. This is done to assert correctness, knowledge, and power. But Dr. Adler praises his children to outsiders—after all, the outsiders don't know his true feelings. Thus he says that his daughter, now married, once had an "important position in Mount Sinai." Miraculously Tommy becomes a success. Underneath his smile, Dr. Adler has lost the "family sense." Tommy, caught between two constructors, wants to shape some ideal construction. He is in love with failure. It is wonderfully ironic that Tommy courts successive losses—in marriage, in his occupation, in his family—in the midst of other crusaders for success. His construction objectifies the actions of Dr. Tamkin and Dr. Adler; his masochism reflects their sadism. But he learns that failure is not the only ideal. He gains self-knowledge.

The transformation of madness in the novel emphasizes again that Bellow's views have changed. Joseph and Asa are more passive constructors than their friends or relatives. They succumb to social regimentation. There is little comedy in their adventures. But Augie and Tommy recognize their potentialities for madness, and they almost miraculously survive. Their opponents—say, a Mrs. Renling or Dr. Tamkin—are funny, less likely to horrify them. Bellow makes madness less Gothic, more humorous.

Look at "The Wrecker." Here the husband is "mad," but his madness is comic. He is obsessively concerned with destroying his home before the city does so. By exaggerating the kind of construction the madman has, Bellow transforms it into humor. The husband is saner than his mother-in-law and the city employee—the others who restrict their behavior. His madness is neither narcissistic, compulsive, nor abstract. The husband knows *why* and *what* he must do. We are for him—for his "poetry," his legendary power, and his magic: "I am a magician. This joint is enchanted, you see. I'm getting rid of a lot of past life, dangerous to the soul." And his wife finally agrees with him: "The best way to preserve the marriage is to destroy the home."

Henderson's madness is similar. He also believes

that he is "considered crazy—and with good reason—moody, rough, tyrannical, and probably mad." Even before his African expedition he does odd things: he speaks to his dead father; he wallows in the mud with his pigs; he screams that the land of Connecticut is contaminated. His expedition becomes obsessive, but the obsession is "good"—he wants to live; he hears his own inner voice saying "*I want*." Each of his adventures becomes a willed act. He must *help* others (as the earlier madmen had to *hurt* others). There are several "ideal constructions" in the novel, but one can serve as an example. Henderson discovers that the water, full of frogs, is no longer good. He decides to get rid of the ugly creatures; unfortunately, his dynamite only blasts out the retaining wall as well as them—the project is destructive. Even so, it is necessary for self-knowledge. (Destruction and construction are linked as in "The Wrecker.") Henderson's madness—benevolent, heroic, but still obsessive—somehow makes him *become* great.

It is possible to look at the themes of *moha* and madness in terms of time. In order to live nobly or even properly, we must not be constrained by the past or the future. We must fight the constructions of our ancestors and Utopian visions. We must seize the day to live "eternally." But even this ideal construction should be flexible—living today implies respect for the wheel of time.

In *Dangling Man* we can see time as a major theme (and image). Joseph suggests that "once upon a time" people kept journals to record their feelings—they "felt no shame." But "nowadays" people are different. He sees a split between the contemporary world and History. Somehow he must fix it. The only way he can do so is by embracing the "eternal return," by living with an awareness of myth. Myth, ritual, eternity—all these heal a restrictive, sick view of time. Because

Joseph wants to live "eternally," he keeps a journal (as people *once* did). In it he uses many mythical references. He likens himself to Siva, hoping that he can have as many mouths as the god has arms, so that he can really talk about his problems. Although he doesn't think of himself as the biblical Joseph, he resembles his ancient "brother" while he lives in a pit (his room), away from his countrymen. When he and Iva go to the party, he says:

> The party blared on inside, and I began to think what a gathering of this sort meant. And it came to me all at once that the human purpose of these occasions had always been to free the charge of feelings in the pent heart; and that, as animals instinctively sought salt or lime, we, too, flew together at this need as we had at Eleusis, with rites and dances, and at other high festivals and corroborees to witness pains and tortures, to give our scorn, hatred, and desire temporary liberty and play. Only we did these things without grace or mystery, lacking the forms for them and, relying on drunkeness, assassinated the Gods in one another and shrieked in vengefulness and hurt.

Joseph thinks of the relationship of ancients and moderns, helping him to establish some deep meanings. He sees proper mystery missing—the absence of "high festival"—but the very fact that he does suggests that he understands the mysterious cycle of time.

But Joseph cannot hold this "eternal" view. Later he returns to a broken conception when he talks to Amos, his brother. Amos looks only at future success, and believes that everyone else should. The *future becomes time*. Joseph cannot accept one aspect—especially the future—as the sole meaning. He cries out: "There is no personal future any more." War, *moha*, madness—these destroy the cyclical flow of time.

So does the neglect of specific moments. Although it may seem that Joseph's neglect of the fleeting days —all days are now "undistinguished, all equal, and it is difficult to tell Tuesday from Saturday"—helps him to regain his eternal view, it destroys this very view. We must be aware of *differences within similarities*, parts within the whole. In his party description Joseph is closer to the truth. He sees present and past, lines in the circle—as he does when he notes: "I always experience a rush of feeling on the twenty-first of March. "Thank heaven, I've made it again!" This is deep knowledge: we must experience the *season of change*.

The Victim contains the same oppositions of time and eternity, abstractionism and mystery. Allbee and Asa don't have any whole view of time because they don't impose proper order on their lives. They see the past, the present, or the future in one-sided, discontinuous ways. They break "connections"—as the phone connection on the first page is broken or the bell of Elena's house is disconnected. The past is the one aspect of time respected—and feared—by the "victims." Allbee is haunted by his lost job, claiming that he was fired because of Asa's "crazy" replies to Rudiger. This past event has assumed overwhelming importance, fragmenting time; it destroys his future. The "original sin," which he cannot understand or accept, also confronts Asa. He discovers dark meanings in the past, disregarding the present and the future. He begins to be haunted by the "curse" of the past. First he remembers the interview with Rudiger, then his dead mother. The fears of *inherited* madness constantly pressure him.

Bellow relates this fear of the past to a deterministic philosophy. Allbee thrusts the philosophy at Asa: "You don't agree that people have a destiny forced on them? Well, that's ridiculous, because they do. And that's all the destiny they get, so they'd better not assume they're running their own show." He constantly repeats the idea of destiny, compelling Asa to think "there was a wrong, a general wrong." Both see currents drowning them—drowning everyone.

One of Asa's dreams emphasizes horrifying determinism. He finds himself in a train station, carrying a heavy suitcase, pushing through the crowd. He has missed the train—the past "overshadows" the present! —but he has another chance to board the train because a "second section of it" is due to leave in three minutes. Asa can still change things and impose order. But when he tries to enter through a certain gate, two men tell him: This gate isn't open to the public. "You can't go back the way you came, either." Asa is pushed into the alley; his face is covered with tears. It seems that "missing the train" is irrevocable.

Because he can see the split between generations, Asa is moving towards an understanding of change, but he sees change as erratic or violent. He thinks of his father once saying how many foreign children, Italian or Irish, died. How strange if his father "could know that his own grandson was one of these, buried in a Catholic cemetery." The last scene suggests that the problem of time remains. Asa sees Allbee no longer depressed, poor, or mad but now "successful." He engages him in a metaphoric conversation about the train. Allbee claims that he is the type that "comes to terms with whoever runs things." He hasn't missed the train; he has adjusted to its scheduled movement. Asa asks: "what's your idea of who runs things?" There is no reply. Bellow suggests that we must accept the past as controlling us—but we should come to terms with it by seizing the day. Only this recovers our freedom.

One way of approaching *The Adventures of Augie March* is by noting "eternal return." Here we find many references to reincarnation, archetypes, frozen movements. These tell us that Augie is not stunted— as are Allbee and Asa, or the various characters in *Dangling Man*—by adherence to one aspect of time. The pattern is set in the first few pages. Augie mentions Heraclitus (a "man's character is his fate"), Timur, Cornwallis. These references broaden the scope—from Chicago, that "somber city," to Greece and revolutionary America. But they also suggest that

Augie as narrator considers the human condition, not simply his own problems. By seeing the ancients in his Chicago relatives and friends, he recognizes that although times have changed, people remain the same. This insight gives him courage and flexibility.

Most critics quote the following passage:

> I'm thinking of the old tale of Croesus, with Einhorn in the unhappy part. First the proud rich man, huffy at Solon, who, right or wrong in their argument over happiness, must have been the visiting Parisian of his day, and condescending to a rich island provincial. I try to think why didn't the warmth of wisdom make Solon softer than I believe he was to the gold-and-jewel-owning semibarbarian. But anyway he was right. And Croesus, who was wrong, taught his lesson with tears to Cyrus, who spared him from the pyre. This old man, through misfortune, became a thinker and mystic and advice-giver. Then Cyrus lost his head to the revengeful queen who ducked it in a skinful of blood and cried. "You wanted blood? Here, drink!" And his crazy son Cambyses inherited Croesus and tried to kill him in Egypt as he had put his own brother to death and wounded the poor bull-calf Apis and made the head-and-body-shaved priests grim. The Crash was Einhorn's Cyrus and the bank failures his pyre, the poolroom his exile from Lydia and the hoodlum Cambyses, whose menace he managed, somehow, to get round.

The passage is funny, of course, but it is also wise. Augie recognizes that Einhorn is "heroic"—like his ancestor, Croesus. He elevates him by the comparison, and lowers the ancient. Perhaps it is better to say that Augie mediates between past and present, recognizing that all times are "wacky" and sad. Thus he echoes Bellow's remark in "The Sealed Treasure": "human greatness can still be seen by us. And it is not a question of the gnat who sees the elephant. We are not members of a different species." [39] By living "eternally," we reclaim greatness from the incredible present.

There are other uses of time in the novel. Bellow not only gives us the eternal return of ancient figures— he presents rituals which suggest a solution to time—a return to the roots of human nature. The rituals stop the flow, helping the characters to achieve a "still point." Anna Coblin, for example, gains pleasure by washing the floors on Friday afternoon. She works carefully, wading barefoot after the strokes of the mop and then spreading papers on the floor. Augie describes this meticulous, stylized "dance" with love—he says that the house is "as regular as a convent parlor or any place where the love of God is made ready for on a base of domestic neatness." Things and human beings are properly related; things don't dominate the "undefended will." Anna asserts the order of the universe, cyclical regularity. (She thus reflects Joseph's attempts in *Dangling Man* to ritualize his daily routine. He polishes his shoes, feeling as "tranquil" and deeply satisfied as he did in the past. The ritual meaningfully connects past and present.)

The Adventures of Augie March is, in effect, one heroic initiation—a massive preparation for "service in the temple." When he and Einhorn go to the brothel, Augie "begins" his sex life. Einhorn becomes the "old wise man" introducing him to the mysteries. Later Augie discovers the natural scene. Sitting in the park, he soaks in the "heavy nourishing air," a "state that lets you rest in your own specific gravity, . . . where you are not subject matter but sit in your nature, tasting original tastes as good as the first man." Initiation also takes the form of the "criminal act"—stealing becomes a ritual with its own forms and mysteries. Augie steals books (as he stole earlier from the department store). He also sees new countries—France, Mexico. All of these initiations reinforce the idea that the "only possessing is of the moment." Initiation never stops, unless one submits to madness and *moha*.

Time plays an important part in *Seize the Day* (as is obvious from the title). Tommy Wilhelm is, at first, a nonbeliever in myth or ritual—the eternal return. He thinks of the past as obsessively as do Joseph and Allbee. He *was once* successful: he *made* a decent living; he *was* happily married; he *was* close to his father. Because he defines himself in relation to a "wonderful past," he has no real future. Like the old men and women in the hotel, he has "nothing to do but wait out the day." Of course, I have simplified the conception. Tommy does have a "future" in the speculation schemes of Dr. Tamkin. Money, success, self-realization—all these wait for him in the stock exchange. But time is not seized by the hero; it is fragmented and idealized. It is actually a *hole* for him.

Dr. Tamkin offers a solution: "The spiritual compensation is what I look for. Bringing people into the here-and-now. The real universe. That's the present moment. The past is no good to us. The future is full of anxiety." Although this solution appears to be vital, it is different from a whole view of time—the one found in Augie's concern with Einhorn as Croesus. Tamkin is also breaking time: the present becomes all-important—which is as bad as Tommy's "backward" vision. We should of course, seize the day, but we should see it as linking all days, as part of a never-ending cycle.

The end of *Seize the Day* suggests that Tommy discovers the "eternal return." After his loss on the stock exchange, he wanders into a funeral parlor. Here it is "dark and cool"—time is forgotten. Only the terrible fact of the human condition is present. Tommy is "past words, past reason, coherence"—past entrapment. He has a vision of *all* men in the coffin and when he sobs incessantly, he is cleansed of his problems. He suffers ecstasy.

In "A Father-to-Be" Rogin sits on the subway seat, thinking of his future son as anonymous, conformist, self-satisfied. Rogin is overly concerned with his vision; he neglects to seize the day until he sees Joan, the woman he loves and hates. The end of the story contains a ritual of cleansing—baptism. Joan, in effect, washes away his sickness by shampooing his hair: "it seemed to him that the water came from within him, it was the warm fluid of his own secret loving spirit overflowing into the sink . . . , and the words he had rehearsed he forgot, and his anger at his son-in-law disappeared altogether." The ritual cleansing—like Joseph's polishing of his shoes or Anna Coblin's polishing of her kitchen—establishes a relationship of individual and environment—a relationship which is "still" and "pure."

"The Wrecker" concentrates on the same sort of ceremony. We first hear the hammering of the husband, and we think that he is completely destructive —he doesn't seem to seize the day. But when he speaks, we know that he is cleansing himself and his wife—in fact, the whole "universe"—by looking at the future in the present: "When there's no demolition there's no advancement. The old must go down. You only see what is built. You forget what had to be taken away, and yet it is the same process. Man does not wait for time to do his work for him." This is the point: we must always rebuild—even rebuild time, imposing our will and intelligence in flexible ways. Then, like the wrecker, we are no longer obsessed by past life, "dangerous to the soul." We fly like the hummingbird he worships.

Now we can appreciate the various rituals in *Henderson the Rain King*. Henderson tries, at first, to accept the past—the money he has is a trophy of history. He uses the money, but it contaminates him. Then he throws it away, ridding himself of the unreal past. He also tries to get in touch with his dead father by playing "Humoresque" on the violin. But again the connection is broken: he gets cramps in his neck and shoulders. Actually the past is death, "So for God's sake make a move, Henderson, put forth effort . . . Because nothing will have been and so nothing will be left. While something still *is—now!*" Finally he tries to get in touch with the "real" past—one different from history or junk. In Africa, past, present, and future have no false meanings; time is lifted for sacred messages. Henderson is near the "original place."

Of course, the simple expedition will not do wonders. When the future rain king attempts to cleanse the water of the frogs, he destroys everything in sight. (The destruction is not as constructive as the Wrecker's ritual.) But he does get closer to the truth. He sees the "strangeness" of things—that strangeness which disrupts benevolent projects. Before Henderson participates in a completely meaningful ritual—embracing eternity—he begins to have more inklings of cyclical movement. He thinks of himself as acting out Daniel's prophecy of the beasts. (Actually Henderson, himself, as Daniel J. Hughes writes, "calls up, either directly or in a parodic mode, Oedipus, Moses, Joseph, Jacob, Falstaff, Lear, etc., and his entire quest has a familiar mythic pattern.") [40] Like Augie thinking of Cornwallis, Croesus, or Columbus, he embraces a view of recurring, ever-present meaning.

The rainmaking ritual is especially important in this context. Why does Bellow use rain? Henderson himself explains: He used to "sing a song in school, 'O Marianina. Come O come and turn us into foam.'" Rain—like the polish of Joseph or Rogin's shampoo—is a cleansing agent; it washes away distractions, various elements of madness. That Henderson is able to lift the god-figure indicates that not only does he embrace divinity, he assumes a new role—he is a rain king, the Sungo. He plays a deep "historical" role—a role which *exalts* him, lifting him out of time.

Henderson carries back this vision to the States. He takes with him Dahfu's lion cub because "the king would want me to take it along. . . . he's got to survive in some form." Dahfu *exists* in the cub as his father exists in the lion. And the new cub is linked to his old bear. When Henderson was younger he loved a bear, Smolak, who—like himself—was an Ishmael—a castaway. He holds the lion cub, seeing in it not only Dahfu but also Smolak. Again time becomes eternal. As he thinks, "You could never convince me that *this was for the first time.*"

If Bellow is constantly aware of the dualities of existence—of *moha* versus spirit, madness versus sanity, time versus eternity—he is "obsessed" with appearances. He suggests that the quest for truth is a difficult, ever-present task—one which must take into account various deceptions. *Moha* does not only fight spirit—it hides it. Madness pretends sanity. The typical quest in Bellow's fiction encounters tricks, acts, confidence games—it can only be successful by engaging in "serious play."

We would expect masquerade from a close reading of Bellow's essays. His "Literary Notes on Khrushchev" suggests: "It's hard to know whether the Khrushchev we saw banging with his shoe at the U.N. Assembly is the 'real' Khrushchev." [41] The Soviet leader is likened to an actor—the "charmer" who doesn't give up the "center of the stage." [42] His politics is "theatre." [43] The West cannot understand Khrushchev's performance because it is not used to play. It remains confused by such "brutal and angry comedy." [44] Other Bellow essays suggest the same theme. In an earlier theatre chronicle he writes: "The actors seem to have no notion of play. I don't know why. Is it too frivolous to play in the theatre? Does it lead to disrespect of their theories? The behavior of the actors is very businesslike." [45] Playgoing should not be for ideas; it should engage us with deception—with what Harold Clurman (quoting Picasso) calls "lies like truth." [46] In an article in *The New York Times Book Review* (February 11, 1962) Bellow suggests again that we Americans devote ourselves to the literal fact, without recognizing the deceptive quality of life.[47] Truth is, after all, more than "objectivity." If we don't see our limitations, we will be like the miner in Alaska: "I have read somewhere that in the early days of the movies a miner in Alaska rushed at the screen to batter down the villain with his shovel." [48] One reason for Bellow's "curious and festive" interview with Joe "Yellow Kid" Weil, an old Chicago confidence man, is now clear: the Yellow Kid delights in play—in the mixture of lies and truth.[49] He is an actor (like Khrushchev) who confounds the system by his art. In fact, Bellow implies that by *recognizing* the pretender —by *being* the pretender—we can see Truth more easily.

Dangling Man contains many references to masquerades. Joseph tells us that people now *hide* their true feelings—contemporary society admits only a "limited kind of candor, a close-mouthed straightforwardness." His own marriage is characterized this way: "We no longer confide in each other; in fact there are many things I could not mention to her." Perhaps the neighbor, Vanaker, functions as the "god" of this false, dark world—like the Army, the entire society outside of the boarding house, he *lurks* in the hall—half-man, half-wolf. Joseph cannot understand his actions—are they sick or purposeful?

Bellow suggests that conversations only introduce more confusion. People pretend to say one thing; their remarks are ambiguous or malicious. Thus Joseph asks his father-in-law how he has managed to remain married to a shrew. The father-in-law recognizes the deep concern expressed, but dodges the question by asking him what he means. Question answers question. Joseph himself should know. We learn that when he worked he had to play different roles—he was a "Machiavellian," "keeping his roles successfully distinct." Father-in-law, son-in-law—all play; all are pretenders of some sort: "Now, he says, all human beings share this to some extent. The child feels that his parents are pretenders; his real father is elsewhere and will some day come to claim him."

Joseph desperately wants to lift the veil; he forces others to do the same. He "conducts a poll"—remember the temporary job Myron offers him. When he sees Burns, an old party friend, who refuses to recognize him, Joseph screams: "Don't you know me? I know you." Although Burns admits recognition, nothing is really accomplished. The lies persist. We now have the party—all the masquerades continue with greater subtlety. Morris Abt's eyes are "quizzical, concealing." He compels Minna to accept his lies when he hypnotizes her. Most critics have disregarded the "party" at Amos' house, but it underlines the pattern I have been tracing. Joseph acts violently: he starts to spank Etta, his niece, after she talks rudely to him. Amos and his wife enter just in time to see the spanking. Etta claims one reason for her uncle's nastiness, which is contradicted by him, but Amos accepts the untruth. Joseph has "additional proof of my inability to read people properly." Or even himself. In his later questioning he inwardly sneers: "You're two-faced. You're not to be trusted, you damned diplomat, you cheat!"

The Victim also contains masquerades—lies, deception, and masks. In the first paragraph we are introduced to the notion of "seems." New York is said to be as hot as Bangkok—the continent "seems to have moved from its place." In this "mysterious" world we have other appearances. Asa cannot understand Elena's remarks about her sick child. Mr. Beard says one thing, meaning another. (The entire business world is filled with pretense. Harkavy, Rudiger, and Williston lie for various reasons.)

Allbee is the chief masquerader. When Asa first sees him, he thinks that he recognizes him: "He has never liked this Allbee, but he had never really thought much about him. How was it, then, that his name came to him so readily?" The appearances increase. Allbee claims to have written a letter asking his "victim" to meet him—Asa doesn't believe him, until he later discovers the letter in his box. Now he must discover the meaning of these various "stunts." *How much is coincidence? How much is planning?*

But he forgets that the world is a stage. Allbee, the actor, performs: "He carried on, giving imitations." Not only does he burlesque Jews at parties; he acts every day with the "usual false note, the note of impersonation in what he did." Perhaps the most "comic" display occurs when he decides to move into his victim's apartment. "You're a lousy counterfeit," says Asa. To which the other replies:

> "Why, you have the whole place to yourself. You can put me up. . . . I wouldn't be inconveniencing you. But if you want me to do this in the right spirit . . ." And to Leventhal's astonishment—he was too confounded when it happened to utter a sound—Allbee sank out of his chair and went to his knees.

Is the performance still going on? Later Allbee wants him to get him a job—not acting but some kind of "movie work."

Even Asa begins to "act." He hides his true feelings —even to himself. Aboard the Staten Island ferry he gazes out on the water "with an appearance of composure, he [does] not look as burdened as he [feels]." He continues to assume a balanced air, fighting the anxiety Allbee's off-centered views give him. He is not the only observer of theatricality. I have already mentioned Schlossberg, who commands the devoted attention of his listeners by equating life and theatre. A good actress, he says, should be a good woman; she cannot merely wear a mask. The mask should be like the face. "Good acting is what is exactly human." Here Schlossberg offers a clue to the many masquerades in the novel. Asa, Allbee, and the others are not exactly human; they neglect their true feelings so much so that they no longer know they are acting. The mask wears them! This is not to deny that life— the stage—will always play with us, challenge us to identify it. *The Victim* ends "with a theatrical hush; the houselights went off. An usher showed them to their seats."

The performance continues in *The Adventures of Augie March*. When we first meet Gramma Lausch, she is instructing the March's to "act" in the dispensary—they must not tell the truth about their financial condition; they must be as delicate as Machiavelli. (Bellow once thought of entitling the novel *Life Among The Machiavellians*.) Grandma Lausch "masked herself up as usual" when she gives advice of any sort—even to Five Properties on getting married. Augie is so used to deception at home that he practices it against society. He becomes a con-man. (Remember Joe Weil!) It is easy for gangsters to take him as an equal.

But Augie doesn't only see—and practice—deception for financial gain. He is an "imposter" when he loves. Before "falling for" Thea, he believes—indeed, forces himself to believe—that he loves Esther Fenchel, her sister. But he has "forged credentials"—he knows he isn't what he seems. He *is* poor, larky, pathetic, weak. Later Mimi tells him to stop deceiving himself: "You try to look more simple than you are, and it isn't honest." Know your capacities for love! Love is, of course, the closest relationship Augie can embrace, and the fact that he is an imposter—as are those around him—brutalizes it, robbing it of its value. Does Thea really love him or herself? Does he really love her or Esther? Does Mimi love Frazer or him? Such questions—are they ever answered?—reverberate throughout the novel. Augie screams at one point: "Dissembling! Why, the master-dissemblers there are around! And if nature made us live and do as worms and beetles do, to escape the ichneumon fly and swindle other enemies by mimicry, and so forth— well, all right!! But that's not our problem." But it is—as the many masquerades demonstrate.

Some critics have discussed in a general way Bellow's concern with masquerades, but they have not looked at the texture of the concern. Consequently, they single out the "artful" con-men, Mintouchian, Kirby Allbee, Einhorn, without recognizing Bellow's use of "theatrical" images in *The Victim* or the "party" performances in *Dangling Man*.[50] I take the masquerade to be a unifying principle in the individual novels.

Consider, for example, *Seize the Day*. The first sentence introduces the idea of concealment—Tommy Wilhelm, we are told, is not less capable than the next fellow in "concealing his troubles." He had once been an actor—like Allbee?—and he continues to act as if he is not in the pit. He smokes a cigar because it is harder to "find out how he feels." Tommy's duplicity—his concern with appearances—is "mainly for his old father's sake." Dr. Adler, as we learn later, insists on hiding his son's failure—and Tommy joins the act.

The idea of masquerade is established by the imagery. The landscape itself changes its appearance. The Hotel Ansonia looks this morning "like the image of itself reflected in deep water, white and cumulous above, with cavernous distortions underneath." Tommy gazes at his reflections in the "glass cupboard full of cigar boxes, among . . . the gold-embossed portraits of famous men, Garcia, Edward the Seventh, Cyrus the Great."

We are now ready for the great duplicity of Dr. Adler and Dr. Tamkin. Dr. Adler tells Mr. Perls that Tommy—or Wilky, his *real* name—is waiting for a good proposition to equal his successful, past job. Adler lies throughout the novel—he refuses to face his own loss of "family sense"—indeed, any idea of failure. Style—deceptive, flashy—counts. But Dr. Tamkin is an even more stylish masquerader. He is the "heroic" Machiavelli. Everything about him is mysterious. When we first see him, we note his concern with appearance. He claims Tommy has an "obsessional look." Because we never know what he really thinks, we are as mystified as the hero, who tries to look at him closely but "gains nothing by the effort." Dr. Tamkin's appearance—as well as attitude—is odd. He uses a "false, disheartening" green ink for his check; he writes in a "peculiar, even monstrous" way. He stands pigeon-toed, a sign perhaps that "he was devious or had much to hide."

And when Dr. Tamkin theorizes, he becomes even more mysterious. He says, for example, that the human bosom contains two souls, the "real soul and the pretender soul." We feed the pretender soul by our lust for material goods. Society, itself, thrives on pretense: "the interest of the pretender soul is the same as the interest of the social life, the society mechanism." Dr. Tamkin maintains that the pretender soul takes away "the energy of the true soul and makes it feeble, like a parasite." Again the charlatan sees the truth—at least partially—of the world, but the very fact that he is himself a pretender towards Tommy (and others) indicates the many appearances around us: True statements by a pathological liar! Tommy, however, accepts the theory, seeing "Tommy" as the pretender soul and "Velvel" as the real soul. Although our poor "slob" is "divided," he gropes toward unity. In the subway, the "dark tunnel," he suddenly sees the "imperfect and lurid-looking people" in a new way. He loves them. And despite his dark vision of the stocks—we are told that he, like old Mr. Rappaport, can't *see* the meaning of the board—he continues to have insight. When he finally stumbles into the funeral parlor, he sees the corpse, and cries for the real soul of everyone.

The masquerade also functions in Bellow's short stories.[51] In "Looking for Mr. Green," which appears in the *Seize the Day* collection, George Grebe looks for Mr. Green so that he can give him his relief check. His expedition symbolizes, in effect, his quest for the real soul. But he discovers that many people in the poor Negro neighborhood consider him as a pretender, a "stranger" because he is white. They don't give him information about Mr. Green's whereabouts, even refusing to acknowledge the man's existence. At last George comes close to the real man, although he doesn't actually see him. He meets a woman who *seems* to be Mrs. Green; her husband *seems* to live upstairs. But he is convinced that there *is* a Mr. Green:

> it was important that there was a real Mr. Green whom they could not keep him from reaching because he seemed to come as an emissary from hostile appearances. And though the self-ridicule was slow to diminish, and his face still blazed with it, he had, nevertheless, a feeling of elation, too. "For after all," he said, "he *could* be found!"

Before he travels to Africa, Henderson lives in a world of masquerades. Although Lily loves him, she must still lie—she tells him in France that her mother is dead. Later she admits that now her mother is *really* dead. Such "con-games"—and there are many more—irritate him. He wants only to capture deep truth. In Africa Henderson discovers at first that if one *looks properly*, he can see reality under appearance—indeed there is no significant difference between the two. *The body is always true.* Queen Willatale informs him that he has a great "capacity" for life, indicated by [his] largeness, and especially [his] nose." Henderson kisses her middle, finding the embrace a "significant experience." This unity of body and soul is also suggested by the spiritualization of *things:* object-world holds spirit-world. Henderson claims that he hears the "voices of objects and colors"; he loses himself (and finds himself) in "practical tasks." (Remember the cleansing rituals in *Dangling Man* and *The Adventures of Augie March*.) He "tricks" life by disregarding dualities. These tricks continue. He speaks more and more about his physical appearance. His face, he tells us, is "always undergoing transformations," but these transformations—these various expressions—are real. They don't hide his spirit; they reveal it. And death, the final end, is revealed by corpses which lack transforming power.

Now Dahfu joins Henderson in dialogues about truth. The same ideas are stressed as before, but they are more "substantial." When Henderson encounters the ruler of the Wairiris, he believes that his previous insights have not yet captured truth. He is assailed by many doubts. Dahfu hints at his "unrest," although his body seems at ease. He is pleasant, but he is savage. Henderson thinks: "But my purpose was to see essentials, only essentials, nothing but essentials, and to guard against hallucinations. Things are not what they seem anyway." Dahfu may be a "con-man."

The savage ruler offers advice: "The world of facts is real, all right, and not to be altered. The physical is all there, and it belongs to science. But then there is the noumenal department, and there we create and create and create." The imagination, he instructs Henderson, can see truth everywhere. But it can also create lies. There is, consequently, no easy solution to masquerades. *They are within us at all times.* But this fact is not "hopeless." Henderson sees that reality is never grasped without hallucinations. One term presupposes the other. *Becoming* is *the vision of both terms.*

Dahfu continues: "Men of most powerful appetite have always been the ones to doubt reality the most." Henderson acknowledges the truth of this remark, largely because he is more overwhelmed by Dahfu's tales of the lion-father which he—as ruler—must capture. Is Dahfu real? he asks. His question plagues him, especially after his dark teacher says: Man "is the master of adaptations. He is the artist of suggestions." (We have come a long way from the masquerades of *The Victim.* Bellow seems here to be saying that masquerades exalt *and* debase us.)

The body-spirit unity which was implied earlier is reemphasized. Dahfu says: "Disease is a speech of the psyche." According to this aphorism, tics reveal inner disturbance; missing teeth reveal missing knowledge, and so on. Such occult knowledge makes Henderson act like a lion—if he can roar, he can be brave! So he is "the beast," assuming the voice and gestures of the lion. Dahfu even partially convinces Henderson that "inanimate objects might have a mental existence." But our rain king still doubts the truth of this astounding remark.

Dahfu has probably read Wilhelm Reich. Reich insists—as do the Christian mystics, at least according to Norman O. Brown [52]—that body and soul are one. The body reveals inner tensions. Here are some typical remarks by Reich: *"Emotion is an expressive plasmatic motion."* [53] *"We work with the expressive language. Only when we have felt the facial expression of the patient are we also in a position to understand it."* [54] It is interesting to note that both Reich and Dahfu— who claim that there are no appearances, *merely realities*—are regarded as "con-men," who further their *own* truth by masquerade.

Henderson learns, after these "conflicting truths," that reality is never grasped. The lion that Dahfu and he assume is the old king, turns out to be another "person." Thus it kills Dahfu. Hypocrisy is very close to Henderson—the consorts desire his life when *he* becomes king. We can consider Henderson's flight from Africa—before they kill him—as another attempt to find truth, despite "the bad stuff . . . coming back." There is no pure truth—without masquerade— as there is no eternal courts of heaven. Becoming doesn't cease—it is always "leaping, leaping, pounding, and tingling."

Many critics have commented on Bellow's Jewishness. Leslie Fiedler insists that we must see it in the larger context: "the Jews for the first time [have moved] into the center of American culture." [55]

> It is the final commentary on our age and on the place the Jew occupies in its imagination, that Huck Finn,

when he returns to our literature not as an item of nostalgia but as an immortal archetype, returns without his overalls, his fishing pole and his freckles, as a Chicago kid making his way among small-time Jewish Machiavellians.[56]

Augie March, for him, is the "most satisfactory character every projected by a Jewish writer in America."[57] Maxwell Geismar, on the other hand, thinks that Bellow has not faced his heritage: "Judaism in [his] work is a source of nostalgia, but also of guilt and anxiety rather than an enlarging or emancipating force."[58] Theodore J. Ross echoes this charge when he states that Bellow by "equating" Jew and Gentile in *The Victim*, refuses to acknowledge basic inequalities and thus remains false to his heritage.[59] Charles I. Glicksberg also notes Bellow's ambivalence.[60]

Bellow himself says very little about Jewishness in his essays. He notes the oddity of David Daiches being a "rabbi's boy in Edinburgh" in his review of *Two Worlds*.[61] He applauds Philip Roth's view of the "swamp of prosperity" that American Jews inhabit.[62] Perhaps his most interesting remarks about his heritage are found in a review of *The Adventure of Mottel the Cantor's Son*.[63] Here he writes: "The Jews of the ghetto found themselves involved in an immense joke. They are divinely designated to be great and yet they were like mice. History was something that *happened* to them; they did not make it."[64] The Jews, he continues, "[decline] to suffer the penalties the world imposes on [them]."[65]

Let us look closely at these two remarks. Bellow is less interested in religion as such—he does not mention laws or rituals—than in vision. For him this vision is *ironic*. Bellow asserts that the ghetto inhabitants were always aware of Janus-faced nature: they were "Chosen" and yet "Rejected"—Chosen By God, Rejected by their society. They learned to value jokes and absurdities.[66] Their own humor reflected the "immense joke of their existence." (In *The Victim* Asa hears a Jewish joke which exemplifies the beautiful absurdity of things: In a little town of Jews, afraid that the "Messiah" would come and miss them, the people build a tower and hire one of the town beggars to sit in it the whole day. "A friend of his meets this beggar and he says, 'How do you like your job, Baruch?' So he says, 'It doesn't pay much, but I think it's steady work.'") The humor is said, expressing a longing for elevation; underneath, it asserts a glad acceptance of divine justice.

We are here dealing with double irony. Bellow's view of his heritage is as ambivalent as he claims the heritage itself is. In his fiction he may use Jewish vision—or irony—but he never confronts it, at least until *Herzog,* except by indirection. Often he avoids it —by masquerading it as something else.

Consider *Dangling Man.* Joseph's predicament is treated as a "personal" situation. We are never really told that he is Jewish or that he has old-world vision. But it is possible to view him as an archetypal Jew who, like Sholom Aleichem's characters, regards existence as the work of a "Religious Humorist." (The phrase is used by Thomas Mann to describe Kafka.) [67]

Joseph thinks of his American society as hardboiled, whereas *he* suffers. It rejects him because he is "different." (Or is it the other way around?) His journal becomes his sole occupation—it is his Talmud; he is a scholar who studies himself rather than divine laws. He tells us little about his appearance, but what he does indicates that he looks Jewish—dark eyes, black hair, straight nose. When Joseph broods about existence, he is more typically Jewish. He wants the Messiah to come in the guise of a "colony of the spirit"— this colony will have "covenants" forbidding "spite, bloodiness, and cruelty." It will be a blessed country— perhaps like the "Israel" of his ancestors. But like Sholom Aleichem's characters (at least according to Bellow), Joseph is trapped.

Joseph's sense of the family is Jewish. Although I consider this aspect of the novel more fully in the next chapter, I want here to note its existence. Family closeness has always been important in Jewish literature—especially the father-son relationship. Joseph tries at all times to be close to his family, but he cannot achieve this little colony of the spirit. He says very little about his own parents—they are "missing" —but he does describe the pomposity and false guidance of his brother, Amos, who instructs him in the ways of the world. Amos is the Jew who has succumbed to the materialistic world—to exile; Joseph remains true to "the craters of the spirit," but he does this with deep skepticism.

Joseph, unlike the ghetto inhabitants, has lost his faith in God. He says at one point: "No, not God, not any divinity. That was anterior, not of my own deriving. I was not so full of pride that I could not accept the existence of something greater than myself." Joseph wants to believe in divinity, but he is so trapped that he can only see it dimly—in a Haydn divertimento. What would his grandfather think of this? Joseph looks for messages not in the Old Testament but in Goethe, *Walden*, Jacob Boehme, Marx, and his own journal.

The hints of Jewishness I have cited—the "alienation," the "Messianic vision," the almost-suffocating family ties, the physical appearance—are less significant than the Jewish humor—sad and hard—pervading the novel. Perhaps this example will suffice: Joseph thinks of his grandfather's photograph, which shows an old man of faith, "his eyes staring and his clothing shroudlike." He remembers that at fourteen he suddenly saw that he would resemble him: "I was upright on my grandfather's bones and the bones of those before him in a temporary loan." Joseph longs for the old faith—the "real Jew"—at the same time that he fears it. When he grows up he meets the "others" who —like Mr. Harscha, the German—stare at him. They also chart resemblances. Thus the grandfather's head —"his streaming beard yellow, sulphurous"—hangs over Joseph, threatening to "devour" him. This example not only holds the Jewish themes—it gives us a clue to Bellow's tensions about his heritage.

The Victim brings these tensions to the surface. Here Bellow emphasizes the various problems he avoided in his first novel. Thus in the first few pages Asa knows that no matter what his beliefs are—is he a believer in God?—he is a Jew to the others. Mr. Beard claims that he is "like the rest of his brethren." Whether he likes it or not, he joins his fellow "victims." The facts that his wife is named Mary and his sister-in-law is Italian no longer matter. There is no real assimilation. He is *trapped* in his heritage. Allbee constantly reminds him of this doom. You Jews aren't violent, he says, but he doesn't use the word "Jew." He knows that Asa will be more upset by guilt—by betrayal—than by anything else. (The Jew, with his belief in colonies of the spirit, his desire to help victims, will always blame himself.) He gives him something to brood about by suggesting that he has victimized a Gentile. Mr. Geismar is surely correct in indicating that Allbee is more Jewish than Asa—more aware of victimization, of blame.[68] He even "delights" in old-world customs, festivals, songs etc., constantly referring to them.

Asa discovers his Jewishness, enacting Sartre's definition in *Anti-Semite and Jew*:

> What is it, then, that serves to keep a semblance of unity in the Jewish community? To reply to this question, we must come back to the idea of *situation*. It is neither their past, their religion, nor their soil that unites the sons of Israel. If they have a common bond, if all of them deserve the name of Jew, it is because they have in common the situation of a Jew, that is, they live in a community that takes them for Jews.[69]

He remembers the "old" ways of his parents—of the Jewish past—only after he is placed into his *situation*. What is ironic is this: New York—the place of alienation—is, to quote Allbee, a "very Jewish city." Bellow suggests that once a Jew is so reminded—*can he remind himself?*—he assumes a historic role; he acts in the way his countrymen have always acted. Asa, for example, suffers more; he feels more guilt; he is more alone. Now we can see one reason for Bellow's ambivalence towards his own Jewishness: like Asa, he seems to resent enacting a role thrust upon him. Being a Jew means for him that he is an "ideal construction" —if not of the Lord, then of the community. Bellow finds it difficult to grow within "anterior" limits.

Because Asa has no real belief in God, he must assert that his present position is the result of chance: "And what more was there for him to say than that his part in it was accidental? At worst an accident, unintentional." He thrusts responsibility onto fate, feeling relieved in being helpless and dumb. Only gradually does he accept universal order—but he doesn't see it as divinely ordained. Things seem to be "exactly human." All men react as he does when placed in *such a situation*—there are no values in a type—be it Jew or Gentile. When Allbee suffers, he resembles Asa; this means that everybody is Jewish (or that nobody is). Bellow does not offer a comforting message in *The Victim*. By showing that Allbee and Asa are exactly human, he implies that Jewishness is less significant than universal truth. He has written a plea for assimilation. But he has not solved the tensions of being a Jew; he has "escaped" from them by loving the world.

The Adventures of Augie March continues this escapist pattern. Although we get a close view of Jewish customs, foods, and proverbs—especially in the early chapters—we don't completely understand the *nature* of Jewishness.

Perhaps Bellow implies that the March family merely accepts historical typecasting—it becomes another masquerade for them. Here is Grandma Lausch: "But she never went to the synagogue, ate bread on Passover, sent Mama to the pork butcher where meat was cheaper, loved canned lobster and other forbidden food, she was not an atheist and free-thinker." But *is* she Jewish? *Why* is she Jewish? Bellow suggests that the family knows that it is "different" only when the "others" say so: "And sometimes we were chased, stoned, bitten, and beat up for Christ-killers, all of us, even Georgie, articled, whether we liked it or not to this mysterious trade." We would expect Augie to resemble Asa Leventhal, but in this "carefree" world he simply admits: "I never had any special grief from it, or brooded, being by and large too larky and boisterous to take it to heart." Anti-semitism needs no more explanation, he continues, than other juvenile delinquency. He even laughs at Anna Coblin's orthodox beliefs: she "had the will of a martyr to carry a mangled head in Paradise till doomsday, in the suffering mothers' band led by Eve and Hannah." She is "silly," directing Augie to the "great eternal things."

Despite the fact that Augie doesn't care about anti-semitism or orthodox rituals, he looks at the world with Jewish irony. Almost any passage indicates his skeptical admiration of greatness. (Rember Bellow's remarks about the immense joke.) When he thinks of Einhorn, for example, he says that he "isn't kidding" as he enters him in the list of great men—along with Caesar, Machiavelli, and Ulysses. Einhorn is great because he is able to endure the onslaughts of existence —endurance is a quality always admired by Jews living in exile. But Augie knows that even endurance can be laughed at: Einhorn, after all, achieves greatness by means of trickery. Endurance and wisdom are not accepted as solemn truths—they are viewed as "cheap items," even by the great men themselves. Think of Augie's attitudes toward Einhorn (and the other great men) in relation to the following "Tale of Chelm":

> In Chelm there once arrived a rich German Jew, a skeptic, who would deliberately ride in his coach each Sabbath, to enrage the villager by his open violation of the Law.

So Chelm sought ways to teach the rich skeptic a lesson. They thought and thought and decided that every Sabbath, when the German skeptic rode through the streets, a few Jews of Chelm would lie down beneath the wheels of his coach, so that it would turn over and he would break his ribs.[70]

The tale suggests that suffering itself can be mocked. Realizing that he cannot achieve greatness for himself, Augie wants only to go his own erratic way. He is a "trader dealing in air," [71] facing life with an "ironic shrug." [72] He is an "anti-hero." Although I have claimed that Bellow doesn't explain Augie's passivity in psychological terms, he does suggest that his hero is "archetypal," *dos kleine menschele.* The little man! How fitting the phrase is! Augie resembles the Jewish folk-character who is "long-suffering, persistent, lovingly ironic." [73] The following description of the "central figure of Yiddish literature" helps us to see Bellow's hero in an old-world way:

> From this central figure of Yiddish literature—one might call him the Representative Man of the *shtetl*—there emerges a number of significant variations and offshoots. One extreme variation is the wise or sainted fool who has often given up the householder's struggle for dignity and thereby acquired the wry perspective of the man on the outside. Another is the ecstatic wanderer, hopeless in this world because so profoundly committed to the other.[74]

The great sense of the *"sanctity of the insulted and the injured"* [75] is always present in Augie's remarks. Here too he follows his Jewish countrymen. He is for the poor versus the silly materialist; he is for his brother, George (the imbecile), his blind mother, and all the crippled. (Indeed, George resembles the child of Yiddish literature: "deprived, yet infinitely loved," as well as foolish—saintly.[76])

The Adventures of Augie March, then, escapes from confronting many problems Jews must face—

how to live in a new world; the right way to approach God—at the same time that it is infused with Jewish humor and legend. It is a strange mixture—perhaps more than any other of Bellow's novels—because it sees Jewishness in a nostalgic, folksy way, disregarding the tensions of *The Victim*. It is dangerous to call it either an American novel *or* a Jewish one. (Perhaps this explains Leslie Fiedler's high regard for it.) [77] It is, paradoxically, unprovincial as it exalts provincial feelings.

Seize the Day is a much more Jewish work, if such a phrase has any meaning; it suggests that Bellow removes his rose-colored glasses and scrutinizes the tensions of Jewish life. He uses the same devices as before, but he is concerned, in part, with probing the *identity* of the Jew in America. *Seize the Day* asks as does *The Victim*: What is a Jew? Why is someone a Jew?

Tommy Wilhelm is torn by his three selves: "Tommy," "Wilky," and "Velvel." Tommy is his desired American self—the good-looking actor who, unfortunately, discovers that he has no real talent and turns to selling products. He is "inauthentic," running away from the old-world. "Wilky" is the name his father calls him—his real name—to control him. Wilky is the bleak, "inescapable self." Bellow reminds us that these names represent two conflicting aspects of Wilhelm's personality—freedom and determinism:

> Wilhelm had always had a great longing to be Tommy. He had never, however, succeeded in feeling like Tommy and in his soul had always remained Wilky. . . . He had cast off his father's name, and with it his father's opinion of him. It was, he knew it was, his bid for liberty, Adler being in his mind the title of the species, Tommy the freedom of the person. But Wilky was his inescapable self.

Wilky knows that he looks like his ancestors—that he has some of their beliefs in the family sense, the sanc-

tity of the insulted and injured, the Messianic vision.
When Wilhelm prays, he resembles the suffering
ghetto inhabitants. But even Wilky may not be his
true soul. He remembers that his grandfather called
him Velvel. Velvel represents the cozy affection of his
heritage. What is interesting, then, is that Bellow uses
three names to symbolize the Jew—Tommy (the as-
similationist), Wilky (the *inescapable heritage*), and
Velvel (the *loved* heritage).

Wilhelm chooses to be Velvel. More and more he
thinks in Jewish terms, finding "power and glory" in
rituals. Old Rappaport asks him at one point whether
he has reserved a seat in the synagogue for Yom Kip-
pur. Although he answers that he hasn't, he expresses
his longing to pray for his dead mother. (He realizes
that he doesn't know the Hebrew words. In the family
structure Grandfather is orthodox, Father has no religion, Mother is "reformed," and he is ambivalent.) At
last he thinks of the Hebrew memorial service—he
begins to resemble his grandfather. And this resemblance is strengthened when he stumbles into a funeral parlor, where a Jewish ceremony is in progress:
"Men in formal clothes and black homburgs strode
softly back and forth on the cork floor . . . The white
of the stained glass was like mother-of-pearl, the blue
of the Star of David like velvet ribbon." Here he
identifies not only with the corpse but with all his
countrymen. He cleanses himself. I assume that his
name is Velvel when he cries.

The surprising thing in Bellow's fiction is that he
does not approach his Jewishness in any consistent
way. *Seize the Day* confronts it more than does *The
Adventures of Augie March*; it is his most *forceful*
acceptance of his heritage—or most *loving* acceptance.
The Victim is, of course, another acceptance, but its
message in effect is an escapist one. We would expect
Bellow's progress to offer another view of the Jewish
theme in his *Henderson the Rain King*. But Henderson is Gentile. He even has a dispute with a Jewish

friend—which compels him out of crazy spite to start raising *pigs*.

The only Jewish vision in *Henderson the Rain King* is indirect—perhaps it lies hidden in the flaming love expressed throughout the novel. Bellow, like his friend Isaac Rosenfeld, seems to accept Reichianism which as Theodore Solotaroff writes, resembles Hassidism. The following statements hold not only for Rosenfeld but for Bellow in *Henderson the Rain King*:

> Rosenfeld was obsessed for many years by the familiar Jewish theme of salvation—or what Harold Rosenberg, in a brilliant reading of Jewish character, has called "the Jewish vertigo." Naturalist that he was, Rosenfeld saw the way out of the underground not through Jewish faith in another, redemptive place, but through the satisfaction of his natural desires. But he was a mystic for all that—and a Jewish one. He tried to bridge the gap between alienation and connection, depression and joy, secularism and transcendence, through the flesh rather than through religious experience, and he found his mentor in Wilhelm Reich. However, Rosenfeld's Reichianism, under the inevitable conditioning of his character, often reads much like Hasidism. "To love all love," he writes at one point in his journal, "even the beloved partner's love for another. For then we see the world spelled out in letters of flame." [78]

What irony! Bellow uses a wealthy Protestant to express a boundless love for the universe. He has come a long way from Asa's victimization. In the wilds of Africa he (as his hero) feels no longer trapped in assuming an historical or cultural role; he expands his Jewishness until it reminds us of Malamud's remark: "All men are Jews." Is such a remark an escape from —or a confrontation of—his heritage?

Bellow's themes are, of course, not so distinct as I have made them. They interact subtly. Masquerades are part of Jewishness; eternity fights *moha* and madness.

Although they are "one," their interaction produces great tensions not only in the characters but in the novels themselves. The final effect, despite Bellow's "larky" tone in *The Adventures of Augie March* and *Henderson the Rain King*, is that of powerful ambivalence.

3

The Characters

It is striking that Bellow always returns to the same characters—the "dangling man," the gambler (or con-man), and the patriarch. Although I have already mentioned these in passing, I plan now to look at them in detail.

The family is at the heart of Bellow's fiction; it is the "holy center" of values. Is it his Jewish heritage which compels him—like other contemporary Jewish-American writers—to see "metaphysical" tensions at home? [1] Perhaps. Family closeness has always been important in Jewish literature, not only in our century but in ancient times. The close relationship of father and son is evident in the biblical lives of Abraham, Isaac, and Jacob. It was expected, of course, that the son would follow in his father's footsteps in the same way the Jews followed the celestial Father. For the Jews the structure of the family incarnated universal structure. Even when rebellious sons asserted their "rights," the kinship of father and son reasserted itself: "O my son Absalom, my son, my son, Absalom! would God I had died for thee, O Absalom, my son, my son!" In the midst of the Jewish family the woman was usually less important. She was shadowy: she took care of the household, but she did not take part in the struggles between father and son. Only in the Jewish literature of the last hundred years does she usurp her traditional role by becoming authoritarian, bossy, meddlesome. [2] Her new role contributes to the already decaying family structure.

This brief sketch suggests some Jewish reasons for Bellow's treatment of the family—his concern with fathers, sons, and the missing woman. But influence of this kind, while significant, is probably less significant than psychological influence. His fictional family no doubt reflects his "first family." My task here, however, is not to regard Bellow as a case history—we know what he thinks of such probing!—but to state once more that his fictional family embraces the themes discussed in Chapter 2.

Only two critics have emphasized the recurrence of fathers and sons in Bellow's fiction. Maxwell Geismar writes: "In this uneasy relationship of father and son (as in the tangled sibling relation of the Jewish 'oppressor' and the anti-Semitic 'victim' earlier) we reach the psychocenter of *Seize the Day*." [3] Leslie Fiedler states that Bellow is concerned with "emotional transactions of males inside the family: brother and brother, son and father—or father-hating son and Machiavellian surrogate father." [4] But these two critics merely hint at the relationships, failing to analyze causes, effects, and parallels.

In *Dangling Man* Joseph has no real concept of the family. He spends much of his time as a bachelor (while Iva works). When he does visit his in-laws, he can't communicate with them. His conversation with his father-in-law, "old Almstadt," is revealing. The old man is "sick," but he makes believe that he is well—"he greeted Joseph with a not wholly ungrudged smile and also as though it might be considered unmanly or unfatherly to fall sick." Son and father are weak—Joseph is stronger, in fact, because he perceives the limitations of Mrs. Almstadt. The important thing, however, is that he wants to have a father to lead him, a spiritual guide, but he can't find one in Mr. Almstadt.

He always acts as son. His relationships with men are uneasy because he views them as potential fathers (and they see him as son); at the same time he resents

their more "powerful," worldly spirit. Many of his
friends and relatives "adopt" him. Myron Adler regards him as a child; he tries to get him a job. Amos
takes "care" of his brother. Of course, it is clear that
they don't understand the "craters" of Joseph's spirit,
but they sense his lack of maturity. They recognize
that he has not grown up.

Now we can explain the various farther-son relationships in social terms: the war situation forces unnatu-
ral roles upon people. But Joseph is a son because of
some deep tensions which he has never resolved. He
says at one point: "The child feels that his parents are
pretenders; his real father is elsewhere and will some
day come to claim him." This statement can be autobiographical: he is in a world of false fathers, searching unconsciously for an *ideal* one. Why should he be
in this position?

Who is the real father? Bellow doesn't present him
fully—again there are only hints. When Joseph visits
Old Almstadt, he thinks that his own father treats
him less considerately than does his father-in-law—
especially about getting a job. His father is an "eaves-
dropper," a "guardian" of the social system. He pre-
fers Amos, who is "alive to his duties"; this older son
reflects his interest in business. Asocial Joseph does
not belong at home.

Because he lacks authority (despite his brooding
wisdom), he continues to do "childish" things. He
reads comic strips. He has fits of violence when he
can't have his way. He asserts power over young ones.
(One ironic incident occurs when a child, holding a
green stick, points it at him, and shoots. The child
becomes, for a crazy moment, a "tyrant.") He tries to
recapture his childhood by remembering his curls,
which were cut when he was four; he links this haircut
to the photograph of his grandfather. The grandfather, who is vividly presented, assumes the role of
tyrant—a much stronger tyrant than the "missing"
father I've already mentioned. Joseph felt at fourteen

(as he does now) that the grandfather would reclaim him, would take his "curls Buster Brown and all."

Perhaps his most significant childish act is talking to himself. His long dialogues with the "Spirit of Alternatives" parallel the "interviews" with his father. *He quizzes himself as his father quizzes him.* Rebelling against his father (as he does against his grandfather and other social guardians), he somehow *resembles* him. He becomes, as it were, his own father, finally throwing a "handful of orange peel at him." But his rebellion is useless without any standards. Torn by rebellion and submission, adulthood and childhood, Joseph decides at last to commit himself. He surrenders to the Army—to the tyrannical father. Before this surrender of "self-determination," he returns to his childhood room—the "fixtures of his youth." The act is symbolic. He senses that in the Army he will be praised for remaining a submissive son.

The Victim is a novel of fathers and sons. We meet the same types: the tyrannical father, the ideal father, the ambivalent son. But they are more fully developed. One epigraph—taken from "The Tale of the Trader and the Jinni"—introduces the father-son relationship as a symbol of guilt and responsibility:

> It is related, O auspicious King, that there was a merchant who had much wealth, and business in various cities. Now on a day he mounted horse and went forth to recover monies in certain towns, and the heat oppressed him; so he sat beneath a tree and, putting his hand into his saddle-bags, he took thence some broken bread and dried dates and began to break fast. When he had ended eating the dates he threw away the stones and lo! an Ifrit appeared, huge of stature and brandishing a drawn sword, wherewith he approached the merchant and said, "Stand up that I may slay thee even as thou slewest my son!" Asked the merchant, "How have I slain thy son?" and he answered, "When thou atest dates and threwest away the stones they struck my son full in the breast as he was walking by, so that he died forthwith."

The wealthy merchant kills a son without realizing it; the Ifrit is heartbroken.

The novel itself—like the epigraph—introduces us to a world of men—women are not very important. Asa Leventhal, like Joseph, is a "bachelor"; his wife, Mary, has gone to visit her family. That he is "single" does not mean that he is not a "father." He finds himself in "care" of his nephew—the sick son of Elena and Max, his missing brother. Micky becomes his charge—symbolically he resembles Asa because they are both "victims" of some "chance" process. The sick son makes him think: "Should someone else —he thought of it seriously—have the right to take the child away? . . . Well, that was the meaning of help-lessness."

Asa also becomes the father of Philip, Mickey's brother. He decides that the boy should spend some time with him in Manhattan. He identifies with this victim, finding in him "something in common." But the "confidence in the understanding between them" fades: "I'm out of touch with kids." Philip is too young to understand the haunted thoughts of his new-found father. When Max returns after Mickey's death to reestablish himself as a responsible parent, Asa instructs him, even though "they had never, since childhood, spent an hour together." He says: Children must be protected. "They were mauled in birth and they straightened as they grew because their bones were soft. Mauled again later, they could recover again." Max—like a child—must be taught to protect himself. Why does Asa deliver this lengthy sermon?

He is a helpless son, alone in a world of tyrannical fathers. We see him in the office at the "mercy" of Mr. Beard and the others who have power and influ-ence. He is somewhat afraid to leave this office for his Staten Island trip. He has always been dependent upon "business fathers": Williston, Harkavy, Dunhill (who sells him a ticket). Occasionally he rebels against them, but the rebellion—like Joseph's fits of violence—is blind. Thus with Rudiger he claims that outsiders haven't a chance for decent jobs because the guild runs everything. He "stands up" to him, ranting for his rights—unaware of his real motives.

Kirby Allbee is, of course, his most important adversary. He is "paternal" because he holds all the authority—even though he seems weak—which Asa fears (and wants—witness his guidance of Mickey, Philip, and Max). Allbee represents, in an ambiguous way, the conscience—the superego. His tales about Rudiger are designed to make Asa suffer with guilt: "I say you're entirely to blame, Leventhal." He forces him to acknowledge the "sanctity of the insulted and injured" —to see his own sinful helplessness.

If Asa is torn by ambivalence, he "loves" Allbee as he "hates" him because the tyrannical father is what he wants to be—at least partially. Consequently, his reactions are confused, misdirected, odd: "Illness, madness, and death were forcing him to confront his fault." The following passage effectively captures his ambivalence:

> But suddenly he had a strange, close consciousness of Allbee, of his face and body, a feeling of intimate nearness such as he had experienced in the zoo when he had imagined himself at Allbee's back, seeing with microscopic fineness the lines in his skin, and the smallest of his hairs, and breathing in his odor. The same sensations were repeated; he could nearly feel the weight of his body and contact of his clothes.

Despite the fact that the passage stresses physical details, it does not suggest latent homosexuality so much as the power-weakness of Asa who, like all of Bellow's sons, cares more about will than sex.[5] Asa "respects" Allbee for torturing him; he likes the tyrant because he shows him that *someone can rule the world.*

There is one incident, however, which forces Asa to strike out at his father. (It is the most dramatic one in the entire novel.) He returns to his apartment to find

Allbee, "naked and ungainly," standing beside a woman who is dressing in haste. I think Asa is upset not only because Allbee has defiled the "marriage bed," but also because he has been "untrue" by sleeping with a woman. The act violates their eternal bond —sex corrupts the "will to power."

We don't get a picture of the real father—there are only hints to suggest his personality. This lack of development limits the novel; surely we need to know more about him so that we can understand Asa's odd relationships. I agree with Richard Chase in this respect:

> What is so far chiefly missing in Bellow's writing is an account of what his heroes want to be free *from*. As Bellow is always showing, their very adaptability lays them open to forms of tyranny—social convention, a job, a father, a lover, a wife, their children, everyone who may want to prey upon them. And all of these forms of tyranny, fraud, and emotional expropriation Bellow describes brilliantly. But only in *Seize the Day* is there a fully adequate dramatically cencentrated image of what the central figure is up against—the institutional, family, and personal fate that he must define himself by, as heroes in the greatest literature define themselves.[6]

The dead father—society's "representative man"—is almost too frightening for Asa to face. But he should face him. So should Bellow.

Here are some passages which describe the dead father. We are told that he owned a small drygoods store. He was a "turbulent man, harsh and selfish toward his sons." Later Asa calls him a "stern, proud old fool with his savage looks, to whom nothing mattered save his advantage and to be freed by money from the power of his enemies." These thoughts pain Asa; he tries to stop thinking. But incidents keep his memories alive. He remembers, for example, his father's remark about the many deaths of foreign children. These details are all we know—they are insufficient to explain Asa's actions in any complete way; however, they do indicate that he has never come to terms with authority. He is ambivalent: he calls his father "stern" and "proud," but *he* would like to have these qualities—and the mess in which he finds himself forces him to see that some pride or sternness would help. The ambivalence he has always felt toward his father colors his reactions toward the other males in the novel—his "paternal" affection for Philip and Max; his "filial" tensions toward Allbee.

It is characteristic of Bellow to introduce an ideal father who tries to help the son adjust. Sometimes the spiritual guide is tricky, but his corruption is less *tyrannical* than the gleeful authoritarianism of an Allbee. Schlossberg is the spiritual guide who, in teaching Asa, offers Bellow's message. This "large old man with a sturdy gray head, hulking shoulders, and a wide, worn face" compels Asa (and us) to be "strongly drawn to him." The attraction is increased when he gives his sermon on the "exactly human" principle: we should be firm—we should not be humble one day and proud the next. "Choose dignity." Of course, the message is a bit superficial, but Asa follows the "spirit," not the "law."

The Victim "resolves" the father-son relationships. Asa does choose some degree of dignity: he accepts his guilt (everyone's guilt) for Kirby Allbee's failures; he understands the reasons for his twisted involvement with authoritarian figures. But the solution to his problems is "lucky." Can he really escape from the dead father? Can he really meet such an ideal guide? Such questions trouble us. Perhaps the false tone is generated fully at the end of the novel; Asa will be a father in a month—Mary is pregnant; things will work out well for the family. But I suspect that his ambivalence toward authority will continue to trouble him as a parent.

In the very first chapter of *The Adventures of Augie March* we are introduced to the "dead" father: "My own parents were not much to me, though I cared for my mother," Augie tells us. His father has disappeared —the sons never mention him, except when Grandma Lausch becomes passionate about money. The entire family then wonders just *what* he was—a sailor, soldier or truck driver? If Augie is right in claiming that a "man's character is his fate" (he quotes Heraclitus), then we would assume that the loss of his real father should force him to act in definite ways. Before Augie can become an adult, he must assert his own masculinity. But what standard of masculinity does he have? There is no father at home; roles are undefined, unbalanced, irregular. I suggest that he becomes very fond of Georgie, his retarded brother, because he sees his own image in him—the helpless child alone in a mysterious world.[7]

Augie easily accepts (at least in part) Simon, his older brother, as a substitute father. This "oriental, bestowing" monarch—like the real fathers of Joseph and Asa—is guardian of the social system, the "money-flow." He teaches Augie about the materialistic ways of the world. Of course, our "son" cannot heed Simon's wisdom—it is not "larky." He must rebel against it, as he does against the other fathers, finding in rebellion a way of striking out at his real father—the first "evil" influence in his life. The loss of his father makes Augie ambivalent towards all the men he ever meets.

He remains a son, lacking the "family sense." His relationships to men—in Chicago, Mexico, etc.—are never satisfactory because he hates and loves them. Of course, he talks more about the *love* he has for an Einhorn or Mintouchian, but this is his way of escaping from confusion. Consider Einhorn as spiritual father. Although Augie thinks of him as the "first superior man I knew," he hints at the inferior qualities of the man—his crippled legs, his "sneaky" deals. Does Augie completely like to carry him to the cat-house? Does he completely like his selfish statesmanship? Obviously not. I do not mean to imply that he goes to the other extreme. The following passage demonstrates his *divided nature*: "Nevertheless I was down on him occasionally, and I said to myself he was nothing—nothing. Selfish, jealous, autocratic, carp-mouth and hypocritical. However, in the end, I every time had high regard for him."

Augie can "resolve" the ambivalence he has—or flee from it—by assuming the role of father. He can be "self-made," no longer dependent upon others who, after all, can't be trusted. (Remember that his own father deserted him.) Becoming a father appeals to him—as it does to Asa Leventhal—because it means that he has captured the missing father in himself. Augie wants, in effect, to be a "catcher in the rye." I have already mentioned his "ideal construction." He tells Clem that he wants to set up a home (one that he has never known?) and take care of kids there. Although he sees only the benevolent aspects of his construction, Clem answers him: You want to be their "holy father." "Your father ditched the family and you did your share of ditching too, so now you want to make up for it." "Holy" paternity is somewhat self-centered.

But he continues to "pore over" unborn children: "I feel I already am a father." When a whore tries to pick him up on the Via Veneto, he claims that he has children. "*Io ho bambini.*" Augie associates this incident with the feelings he gets from the painting of *Les Orphelines*: the painting makes him cry.

The Adventures of Augie March is a "private" novel. But Bellow shows us that the search for a father helps to explain the great actions of history. Augie's confusion is "classical." He thinks of his real father as a "marble-legged Olympian," of Einhorn as a Caesar, Ulysses, or Sun King in Versailles, of himself as an Eli in the temple or a "sort of Columbus." These references (and there are many more) reinforce the idea that history is "personal." Wars, discoveries, projects

—all these result from tensions of fathers and sons. Bellow is not "loony" in this respect. We need only cite such works of cultural history as *Totem and Taboo* or *Young Man Luther* to prove that he follows many modern thinkers.[8] *The Adventures of Augie March* resembles *Joseph and His Brothers, Ulysses,* and *Absalom, Absalom!*—representative modern novels—in asserting that fathers and sons fight in archetypal ways. Augie's problems are our problems: How can we accept the lessons of history? How can we be "traditional" and progressive?

Seize the Day is a more powerful work because, as Richard Chase suggests, it offers a complete, dramatic confrontation of father and son. Here the real father, Dr. Adler, is no longer shadowy: we *see* his stern and proud character—not only when Tommy directly confronts him but throughout the short novel. The father is always present, lurking in his son's thoughts. Thus Tommy worries about his appearance "mainly for his old father's sake." He then tells us that his father, although "affable," inhibits his freedom; he doesn't even lend a helping hand. Dr. Adler has lost his "*family sense.*" Of course, the neighbors don't know this: they simply accept the old man as a good provider who loves his children and brags about them. Dr. Adler is not wholly evil. Although he is self-centered, he does care about his son's "mixed-up" life. But he believes that he should not help him—Tommy, after all, is middle-aged, sloppy, weak, and clumsy. He can't tolerate the oxlike actions of his son: "Why can't he stand still when we're talking?"

Tommy does not see the ambivalence of his father toward him—he sees only one side. In contrast to Asa or Augie, he constantly thinks of the family. The problem is that he is a weak son surrounded by mysterious fathers. The pattern is set at the beginning. When Tommy chats with Mr. Rubin, the clerk, he finds that he assumes his usual filial role. The old man, who is dressed well, tells him: "You're looking well."

Tommy responds "gladly." What we have, then, is an eager child hoping for paternal love of any kind—love which will acknowledge his existence. Bellow, ironically enough, has his hero live in a hotel full of old people—possible replacements for Dr. Adler. The whole world of upper Broadway reinforces Tommy's search for a father.

Although Tommy is looking for a substitute father, he does not realize that anyone he finds will be imperfect—will, in fact, create the same tensions Dr. Adler does—because he has never solved his ambivalence. He hates his father because he is a "self-made" man; at the same time he respects and even loves him for such strength of will. It is useless to bid for liberty with a new name as he does—the inescapable ambivalence remains. That is why we discover that Tommy cannot believe in free choice. He rationalizes his lack of self-determination (in regard to his fathers) by saying:

> Then it came over you that from one grandfather you had inherited such and such a head of hair which looks like honey when it whitens or sugars in the jar; from another, broad thick shoulders; an oddity of speech from one uncle, and small teeth from another.

Tommy accepts Dr. Tamkin as a spiritual guide, largely because the man holds "secret knowledge." Although many critics have seen this charlatan as another Allbee—a slightly corrupt guide—they have not indicated why he is so attractive. Tommy admires his knowledge about the family; he hopes to pattern himself after such a "family man." Dr. Tamkin nods knowingly when he hears his "son" say: "I had some words with my dad." He answers: "It's the eternal same story . . . The elemental conflict of parent and child. It won't end, even. Even with a fine old gentleman like your dad." Then he adds: you should be proud of such a "fine old patriarch." Tommy sees Tamkin as a father who understands the relationship of fathers and sons. Of course, he discovers that his ideal father is as evil—narcissistic, materialistic—as Dr. Adler. But he still loves him. Unconsciously, he can't live without such tyranny—he wants to remain "castrated."

Tommy would also like to be a father to his sons. When Tamkin forces him to admit that he loves Dr. Adler, Tommy gasps and thinks of his two sons who live with his wife, Margaret. He wants to be with them —to take them to Ebbets Field, to tell them jokes. Thus he resembles Asa and Augie in this respect.

The family sense—filled with conflict—is Tommy's curse *and* blessing. Gradually he widens his view of life to embrace not only fathers and sons—but "brothers" and "sisters." He looks at all people as his relatives. In the subway tunnel he "blazes" with love, thinking that the "lurid-looking people" near him are his brothers and sisters. There is a larger family—there "sons and fathers are themselves." At the end of his adventure (his "old life") Tommy embraces the family again when he mourns for the corpse in the parlor —the corpse is not only himself but Tommy and Paul (his sons), Dr. Adler—everyone. The other mourners wonder whether he is a cousin or brother. They don't realize that he has finally found his father and himself —humanity—in the coffin. The "great and happy oblivion of tears" results, then, from the family sense which Tommy could not neglect—his love is "great" as is the greatness of the heroes mentioned by Augie March. Bellow is not, therefore, so interested in Oedipus complexes, castration and the like as he is in metaphysical overtones. Again he puts his fathers and sons in the center of the universe—their conflicts must continue if they want to seize truth.

In "A Father-To-Be" Rogin, the young chemist, broods about existence as he travels on the subway. He gazes at the people sitting next to him, wondering about their family ties. He sees a dwarf sitting with his mother, a middle-aged man who is "sturdy, with clear skin and blue eyes," and a small girl. For a moment he is flooded with love. Then a strange thing occurs. The middle-aged man—a dull business-man?—begins to resemble the hero's girl friend, Joan, and her father. He even becomes an image of a son. The latter image primarily disturbs Rogin: "Rogin was frightened and moved. 'My son! My son!' he said to himself, and the pity of it almost made him burst into tears." The father-son relationship is one of differences, misunderstandings, and hostility. "Father and son had no sign to make to each other." Despite his fear of the middle-aged man sitting next to him. Rogin sees that he should not be alarmed because *he* after all, looks like him. The family roles are, in other words, so confusing to Bellow's hero that he cannot cope with them. He flees from such anxiety, finding some degree of peace when he is finally embraced by Joan who calls him "baby."

Like Tommy Wilhelm and Rogin, Henderson is involved with many fathers. He tells us about his real father: "He could not settle into a quiet life either. Sometimes he was very hard on Mama; once he made her lie prostrate in her nightgown at the door of his room for two weeks before he would forgive her silly words." The elder Henderson, it seems, is somewhat tyrannical. As usual, Bellow gives us little information about the real father—simply these hints of strength and pride. The significant thing is that Henderson wants to capture his father who is dead; he plays his violin: "Oh, Father, Pa. Do you recognize the sounds? This is me, Gene, on your violin, trying to reach you."

Trying to reach you. Henderson continues his quest. When he says, *"I want, I want, I want,"* he is speaking to his father. In Africa he discovers many substitutes for parental authority—they are ideal like Mr. Schlossberg or, better yet, Dr. Tamkin. They have occult knowledge; they "understand" the laws of the universe. Look, for example, at Willatale. She is a "Bittah"—that is, a "person of real substance. . . , not

only a woman but a man at the same time." She knows
that his heart is breaking, but she tells him that such
feeling is part of his "capacity" for life. She even
recognizes that he is a child. The latter bit of information astounds him: "All my decay has taken place
upon a child." He is a child because life continues to
be "wonderful" for him.

Now the previous father-son relationships which
were particularly painful are transformed. Henderson
—unlike Augie or Asa—recognizes *his own childish-
ness and thrives on it* (as he does on his similarity to
the "loony ancestors.") He is "more at home" in a
world of mysterious strangers. When he meets Dahfu,
he does not view him with as much alarm as would the
earlier sons. The ruler of the Wariri, again, has secret
knowledge, but he is not awe-inspiring. He, too, is
searching for his father—in the form of a lion. The
reconciliation of father and son hinted at in *Seize the
Day* is more fully achieved here because Henderson
and Dahfu (son and father) both understand the ne-
cessity of love: they echo the thought: "For every son
expects and every father wishes to provide clear principles. And moreover a man wants to protect his children from the bitterness of things if he can."

One of the rituals suggests the underlying tone of
the father-son relationships in the entire novel. The
gods—the tribe's fathers—don't look like a "stern
bunch," but they do have dignity—mystery: after all,
they rule everything. It is a necessary fact of life that
their children, the Wariri, should move them, thereby
asserting their own power. Henderson participates in
the ritual, moving Mummah who, although a god
seems a "living personality, not an idol." He thus
becomes the rain king, assuming a historic role or
presence. Gods and men, tradition and "progress"—
these don't violently disagree. But this does not mean
that fathers and sons are ever *completely* united. Henderson distrusts the secret knowledge of his ideal
guide, Dahfu. Dahfu, himself, mistakes one lion for

the true one—his father—and he is killed. Humanity never seems to possess that redeeming love which unites opposites—except at rare moments.

Henderson's love of children is even greater than his love of fathers. Throughout his adventures he babbles about kids, seeing in them his own image. Before he leaves for Africa, he admires Ricey's colored child, feeling for a second that he is Pharoh seeing little Moses. When he arrives in the Arnewi community, he regrets not having taken some "treats for the children." He thinks constantly of his twin boys who are four years old—he must get them a dog.

Finally we have a scene which momentarily unites sons and fathers. On the plane home Henderson adopts an orphan, who begins to play with the lion cub—the "spirit" of Dahfu. He looks at his ideal son and father; their wonderful game reflects his own relationship to the elder Mr. Henderson. The scene is mythic: Henderson knows that fathers and sons— fighting and loving—can never be separated. Consequently, he more than any of Bellow's heroes, except perhaps for Tommy Wilhelm and Moses Herzog (as we shall see) reaffirms that he is truly a family man.

Bellow characterizes women less adequately than he does fathers and sons; they are nonsubstantial, except when they pursue or assert power.

Dangling Man demonstrates the role of women in all of Bellow's fiction. Although Iva is married to Joseph, we see little of her (even in his thoughts). She is working to support him: "She claims that it is no burden and that she wants me to enjoy this liberty, to read and do all the delightful things I will be unable to do in the Army." But she is *missing*; she doesn't exist for Joseph as much as do his "fathers." He wants her to be away. He is "afraid" of any strength on her part, of any individuality. When they go to the party, he commands her—as he cannot command the men around him—to stop drinking. But she disobeys; she asserts her will and gets drunk. This rebellion is relatively minor. Later Joseph tells us more about his "better half":

> Iva and I had not been getting along well. I don't think the fault was entirely hers. I had dominated her for years; she was now capable of rebelling (as, for example, at the Servatius party). . . . Was it possible that she should not want to be guided, formed by me?

He wants Iva to be subject to his strength (or weakness). He can assert what little will he has over her.

But the passive Iva *as a woman* cares little about such struggles. She lives in her own world of "clothes, appearance, furniture, light entertainment, mystery stories, the attractions of fashion magazines, the radio, the enjoyable evening. What could one say to them?" Joseph cannot communicate with such a materialist, especially when she rejects his irresponsible behavior.

The other women in the novel are, similarly, not fully drawn. But they do supply anxiety—the more alive they become, the more dangerous they are! Iva's mother, Mrs. Almstadt, is the "usual" mother-in-law. She is rather bossy as she takes care of her sick husband and her silly son-in-law. Joseph resents her, calling her vain, stupid, and proud—he is, in an odd way, afraid of her. Thus he must convince his father-in-law that he should fight her, assume the dominant role. *They* should not allow her to be equal. *They* should not be "dog-like." Marriage should be more than "babble, tedium and all the rest"; it should be a masculine protest.

When Joseph visits his sister-in-law, he carries his power-weakness complex with him. Although he admires Dolly's graceful neck, he dislikes any strength she possesses. Women, again, are to be beautiful and earthy; they should not get in the way. He especially dislikes Dolly's daughter, Etta, a vain girl who has as many tantrums as he does. Etta, in fact, is the most dangerous woman in the entire novel. She carries the idea of rebellion the farthest, insisting that he *obey her*. She tells him that he must stop playing his Haydn record. She invades his spiritual world. He becomes very angry and spanks her. I suggest that, in effect, the spanking symbolizes the basic hostility he has toward all women—a hostility which is fearful at the same time.

Joseph has one love affair. He finds peace with Kitty because she is not "intelligent or even clever." She yields to him; she is a kind of pet—unassertive, soft. But she also asserts her will by asking him to leave Iva. The situation is ironic: all women, even those who, like Kitty, are loose, want marriage and force men into it. When Joseph refuses to obey, she cares less for him. She begins to see other men. He then finds himself "ambiguously resentful and insulted."

Ambiguity, tension, ambivalence—these words describe Joseph's relationships with women. Why should he fear—and hate—their equality? Bellow supplies some causes. Joseph thinks rarely of the first woman he ever knew—his mother. When he does, he remembers that she disliked cutting his curls (he was four); she finally obeyed her sister, Dina, a "self-willed" woman, and allowed the haircut. Later he remembers his mother's death—just the death itself, not her last words. These two glimpses of the mother are the only ones we have. Do they tell us anything? Perhaps. Joseph misses her, finding her a source of comfort. She treated him as a cute little boy; she pampered him so much that he had no problems of will with her. But the fact of her death meant that he could no longer belong to his mother. He had to stand alone. Standing alone was so precarious, however, that he could not cope with it. He wanted an understanding woman who could solve his problems. He didn't find any—only grasping, barbaric creatures. That is why his mother remains as an ideal, a pure housewife. When Joseph gazes at Marie, the maid, polishing the windows, he recaptures his mother, for only a moment:

> I sat watching Marie this morning as she changed the sheets and dusted and washed the windows. To see her at the windows fascinated me especially. . . .
>
> To make a dirty surface clean—a very simple, very human matter. I, while shining shoes, grew partly aware of it. In those moments at the window, how different Marie was, how purely human as she rubbed the glass. I sometimes wonder if it can be entirely a source of pleasure to clean. . . . But it has its importance as a notion of center, of balance, of order. A woman learns it in the kitchens of her childhood, and it branches out from sinks, windows, table tops, to the faces and hands of children, and then it may become, as it does for some women, part of the nature of God.

Asa Leventhal's marriage to Mary is odd. She is as shadowy as Iva; she is *absent* during the novel. We know her only through her husband's thoughts, but what little information he gives us is intriguing. It seems that she married him because of "true love." When they first met, she was a beautiful woman running at a picnic; she was awkward, unaware that she "was a woman." She spoke freely, charming Asa who was insecure enough to feel that she saw his weakness. But he was lucky. Mary's weakness was greater than his: she was confused not only about herself as a woman but as a wife-to-be. They were married. The reasons for the union are clear: Asa married her because it comforted him to have some power over her; he asserted what little strength he had over someone else. But at the same time she gave him strength. *She finally took care of him.*

Because Asa is so unsure of his role as "son," he continues to look at Mary as powerful, not as physically attractive. He is ambivalent towards her, but he cannot do without her. This is why Allbee's game disturbs him: if Mary were home, he would not be as terrified as he is now. Asa constantly hopes that he will hear from her—that she can take care of the situation. (He is perhaps more clearly "son-like" towards his wife than Joseph is towards Iva.) But she remains off-stage like a goddess. Allbee, I take it, is shrewd enough to see his victim's dependence, and he hints at dark possibilities of loss—remember, he warns, that his own wife had died; look what has happened to him! Such threats make Asa long even more for Mary's "ability to restore normalcy" (as does Marie?). After she does return—we never see the reunion—she presumably calms him. Years later she becomes pregnant. Characteristically, she instructs him to go to the theater with her even though he says it is too warm to go. He offers no real opposition because he sees her now as a mother. Is he her child?

Juxtaposed to Asa's dependence upon Mary is his hostility—and fear—towards "crazy" women. Elena, his sister-in-law, is more erratic and willful than Mary. All her actions proclaim disorder: she can't care for her sick son, Mickey; she can't keep her house clean; she has what he calls "superfluous energy in her movements." Asa dislikes her *unpredictable behavior*. It frightens him because he sees that it is part of his nature. He sees his own "madness" in Elena.

Look closely at his thoughts. Asa wonders "what could [he] do with Elena?" She is so loony that she should not be a mother. She reminds him of his own mother, whom he remembers "faintly." Like Bellow's other "parents," she is a vague figure. But here we learn one important fact: Asa's mother was insane, at least according to his father. When the son looks at other women—especially distracted ones—he sees his mother: "it gave him a clearer view of each of the women to consider that they were perhaps alike." Thus he probably sees in Mary an ideal figure, one who, by being "sane," can become the mother he never knew. But Asa, at the same time, cannot allow anyone to be his parent. "Parents!" he mutters. In that strange scene when he sees Allbee and the whore, he attacks his tyrannical father. Secretly he likes him for corrupting the marriage bed, Mary's "presence." Allbee has attacked the family sense; this is what Asa would like to do. But he must hide his feelings—after all, what would Mary think! Although *The Victim* ends with the triumphant return of the ideal, I think Asa continues to be a victim of unceasing ambivalence.

Between *The Victim* and *The Adventures of Augie March* Bellow published two relatively minor stories in *Harper's Bazaar*: "Dora" (November, 1949) and "By the Rock Wall" (April, 1951). Both offer interesting characterizations of women.

Dora resembles the Marie of *Dangling Man*. She is a servant—homely, unintellectual, unmarried. But she *cares* about people; she doesn't regard herself as superior or bossy. When her neighbor has a heart attack, she takes care of him until the ambulance arrives. Then she visits him every day. Bellow respects Dora because she is a creative person who establishes order —not only in her cleaning rituals but in these benevolent actions. But she is a *less complex woman* than we expect, emerging, finally, as a kind of stupid ideal. How would she act as a wife? Would she remain the same? Is she "exactly human?"

"By the Rock Wall" is a story about marriage. The hero, Willard, learns from his wife that she was unfaithful to him fifteen years ago. This discovery makes him see that "during years of marriage you eat with, speak with, bear with, share a bed with, a woman, and yet at last you have to admit that you have worked out a manner of dealing with each other as with all others, like casually connected people." He and she must overcome their casual connection. But this task is difficult. Their years of marriage have been tests of will —she used to cross-examine him, go through his mail, be rude to other women who spoke to him. Although he outwardly hated such persecution, he secretly desired it. His wife was predictable; marriage was se-

curely unpleasant. Now that they admit their infideli-
ties—for Willard too has had misdemeanors—they
must face their new precarious position. He must see
his "impulse of softness"; she has to live with her
active will. They must see that their marriage has been
a "swindle": "He had banked on her, having secretly
given himself up, and she, too, was swindled."

With their added knowledge, they do become rec-
onciled to marriage as a "war of love," and to their
own dark natures. But they still are separated:

> Meanwhile—and he thought that this must be true
> for her, too—there were certain things of which he had
> strong possession, which he could not tell her of, which
> she could not tell him of, which were ineradicable
> and which remained in his flesh, and which he had no
> final wish to give up even though he loved his wife and
> was aware that a reconciliation was coming.

Marriage implies divorce.

Augie March joins the other ambivalent sons. His
real mother is "simple-minded" and completely passive. He cannot have any deep respect for her because
she is less of a parent than a child. Grandma Lausch,
on the other hand, is tyrannical—she governs everyone
like a "sovereign." In fact, she becomes Augie's
mother (and father), teaching him about the ways of
the world: corruption, pride, and masquerade. The
consequences of having two mothers deeply affect
Augie, who grows up thinking of women as weak or
strong. He goes out of his way—or is forced to by
Bellow—to meet other disturbing creatures more intent upon their will to power than love.

Anna Coblin is, like Grandma Lausch, a tyrannical
woman who decides to treat him as her "own boy."
She tries to mold his unformed but already ambivalent
nature, offering him religion, feasts, and strict order.
Augie resents order in his later years because he sees it
as "maternal"—something Grandma Lausch and
Anna respect. It destroys a "son's" freedom of move-

ment. He is rebelling, like Huck Finn, against the righteous women around him. (Although I don't want to pursue the parallel, there are interesting similarities between Huck and Augie as sons: both are dominated by strong, proud women; both lack "fathers" at first; both are confused about rebellion and acceptance of the family.) But these authoritarian women continue to smile at him, making his existence itself a "test of strength."

There is Mrs. Renling, "pushing fifty-five," who "plays terribly on [his] vanity," giving him proper clothing, riding lessons, good food—all the while she regards him as a son who can be *perfected*. Her noble concentration—her leadership—confuses Augie. He almost succumbs to it, wanting to remain a submissive, cute child—after all, his troubles would then be over!—but he finally asserts what little will he has, and he fights his new mother. One interesting aspect of their relationship comes across: there is a mutual "physical" attraction. Does Augie find Mrs. Renling attractive because she is "foreign?" Or does he somehow find her will attractive? Does she love him because he is handsome or weak? Such questions are raised by their relationship as they are raised again when Augie meets Thea.[9] Bellow does not answer them.

Thea Fenchel is beautiful, but Augie is more aware of her "hot, prompt, investigative, and nearly imploring face." He sees her "strong nerve," her "recklessness" that gives "as much concern as admiration." She pursues him, although he "loves" her sister, Esther, at first. Finally she wins him, taking him along, to Mexico: "She assumed that I'd go to Mexico with her." She *assumes many things, believing that her will is supreme*. Gradually Augie begins to sense that he is a "slave": "So why hunt for still more ways to lose liberty?" he asks himself. He understands that he "could not find [himself] in love without it should have some peculiarity."

Thea's peculiarity is obvious in the eagle-taming incidents. "Caligula," as he names the eagle, becomes her *"idée fixe,* almost child." She insists upon breaking the bird's will as she teaches it to hunt. Augie doesn't want to touch the bird out of a dim awareness of "brotherhood." Then he does instruct it, hoping to show himself and Thea that he is "different" in being stronger than Caligula. But an accident makes him accept his dark motives: he then breaks his relationship with Thea. Of course, the entire incident is Lawrentian—as most critics suggest—but not for the superficial reasons. The war of Thea and Augie—of which the eagle-taming is a mere reflection—resembles the will to power in *The Fox* or *Sons and Lovers*: authoritarianism is "sexual."

Augie next falls in love with Stella who, like Joseph's Kitty, is passive. She looks at him as an image of wise strength—a "father"—and accepts his scheme for the foster home. However, she is a materialist. Thus she is as "different" from Augie as "natural" Thea. He can accept her elegance as long as she obeys his commands. Unfortunately, the more successful she becomes—she is a starlet!—the more power she has. She then exists in a world Augie can't reach—a world of power and money. Their marriage is unbalanced: Stella becomes an independent child (simple and deceptive); Augie cannot *boss* her and—more important—cannot obey her. Therefore, there is an impasse; another love affair is "indeed cockeyed."

Perhaps Augie's most satisfying affair is with Sophie. This Greek girl is completely passive, cozy, submissive—he is able to feel more comfortable with her than with the other women he meets. His masculinity —which was constantly threatened by Mrs. Renling and Thea—reasserts itself: he is an *idol* for her. But Thea comes along to destroy their pure relationship.

The love adventures of Augie March are generally inconclusive, unbalanced, odd. They show us that his character is his fate—that character formed, without his knowledge, by authoritarian Grandma Lausch and his weak mother. He never does relate these separate images; he continues to be plagued by them. He is a "flop" as a lover.

Tommy Wilhelm is also a flop. His wife, Margaret, refuses to grant him a divorce; he has to give her and the two children more money than he can afford. She bosses him—like Bellow's other authoritarian women—telling him neither to send postdated checks nor to skip any payments. She "hits" him—"she seems to live for that alone," Tommy complains to his father. Why should Tommy get into this position? Why should he be "in the dark" when it comes to women? These questions are not answered. We know so little of Tommy's mother that we cannot even hazard a guess about her role in his character-formation. He mentions her a few times, refusing to think of her at any length. One of his remarks seems to be important. His mother was the one who tried to stop his acting career —"Poor Mother" was hurt by his failure. Tommy regards her as an ideal—perhaps he can never find any woman to equal her.

In a way Dr. Tamkin's remarks about women hit home:

> "Innately, the female knows how to cripple by sickening a man with guilt. It is a very special destruct, and she sends her curse to make a fellow impotent. As if she says, 'Unless I allow it, you will never be a man.' But men like my old dad or Mr. Rappaport answers, 'Woman, what art thou to me?' You can't do that yet."

Tommy does regard Margaret as a castrating woman —a woman who demands not only to be equal but to be superior. (She is another career woman like Iva, Stella, or Mary.) The only way she can assume her new role is by hurting him and her sons. The irresolution of Tommy "disappears" when he weeps for humanity, but I think it will reassert itself in any future marriage.

Joan in "A Father-to-Be" is another "modern"

woman. She tells Rogin what to buy at the store; she spends his money recklessly. She refuses to be a mere stay-at-home, washing dishes, mopping floors (like the ideal women in Bellow's fiction). She even sees a psychiatrist. Although Rogin hates her destructive tendencies—will she really take away his masculinity? —he thinks of her as a mother who takes care of him. His own mother had always spoiled him, never even allowing him to cut his own meat. Because Rogin is so weak, he likes Joan's self-assertive commands, and finds final happiness in her "wonderful ideas." He kneels in admiration of her "regular gift"—her will.

Even in "Looking for Mr. Green" the woman is the strong creature who holds Grebe's fate. She stands between him and Mr. Green (her husband or father?), asking him: What do you want? She yells at him, forcing him to hand over the relief check. The "madness" of this scene emphasizes again the eternal power of Bellow's women.

"The Wrecker" views the tensions between men and women in a comic way. The mother-in-law and wife are both meddlesome—they are sane, they claim, and consequently they must take control of the situation, shaping it to their normal ends: "A man who has no respect for a thousand dollars isn't intelligent. You're ascared to do better in life." They see the wrecker-husband as a "boy." But he sees them as bossy fools who don't understand higher things than money —such things as the ecstasy of destruction: "Only the most ordinary men should become husbands. Whatever they may dream of, when you come right down to it women want their husbands to be ordinary and to make no trouble." He continues: "Husbands are not heroes." (Thus he echoes Augie, Joseph, and Tommy). Of course, in this comedy, the women don't win—they don't succeed in castrating him. The wrecker, moreover, convinces his wife that his task is heroic: she joins him in destroying conventional patterns.

The joy expressed in this one-act play is echoed in

Henderson the Rain King. Although Henderson cannot get along well with Frances—she divorces him—he does manage to achieve a "happy" second marriage with Lily. What sort of woman is she? She is relatively passive before Henderson's mad onslaughts. She accepts his odd social behavior—he treats her as a stranger at parties—with calm understanding. But her actions are *too* calm to be fully appreciated; sometimes they are strong-willed, disturbing her husband, who says: "I treated her like a stranger before the guests because I didn't like to see her behave and carry on like the lady of the house; . . . she is not a lady but merely my wife—merely my wife." He tries to upset her balance, by threatening to shoot himself as her father did.

The interesting thing about their marriage is the difference in age: Lily is twenty years younger than Henderson. She is a daughter to him—remember his "will to fatherhood." The unbalance in age reinforces —or causes—their funny battles. Occasionally Lily wins: she then moralizes, telling her husband to "straighten himself out." Henderson simply asserts his power by more mad behavior.

The Wrecker claims that "heroes are not husbands." So does Henderson. Despite the liveliness of his battles with Lily—his tests of hardihood—he is bored: "Family life with Lily was not all that might have been predicted by an optimist, but I'm sure that she got more than she had bargained for, too." When he describes his typical day of marriage, we see that he is really "divorced." Lily gets into the convertible with the twins and drives away; he stays at home, trying to reach his dead father. Is it any wonder, he asks, that he has to go to Africa?

Henderson does not meet many women in Africa—the ones he does meet are, like Lily, "types" or curiosities. The first is Queen Willatale, an elderly lady full of "good nature." She knows everything about Henderson. Unlike his young wife, she understands that he *wants*, he *wants*. The ideal wisdom of womanhood—perhaps like Marie or Anna Coblin in their cleaning rituals—is embodied in Willatale. But she doesn't emerge as a person—after all, she is supposedly more than a mere person! Her sister Mtalba cares little about Henderson's spiritual longings: she only admires his body. But she is even more of a caricature than Willatale. We laugh at her "mammoth" body and desires. The other women—of the Wariri tribe—are the naked "amazons" who guard and cater to Dahfu. They are voluptuous, submissive, and a bit ominous.

Henderson cannot stop thinking of Lily. When he becomes the Sungo, he wonders how he can tell her about this new role. He thinks of Dahfu as a moralizer like Lily. As he tells us: "I dearly love that big broad." Later he composes a letter to Lily, informing her of all his explosive feelings. But at the same time he thinks: *"What have I got to do with husbands' love or wives' love? I am too peculiar for that kind of stuff."*

This thought bears repeating: Henderson—like all of Bellow's heroes—is *too peculiar for that kind of stuff*. They regard women, in general, as inferior, non-spiritual creatures. Although they appreciate female beauty, they think of it less frequently than power. Usually they are ambivalent: they want to be dominated and/or to dominate; marriage is always a struggle for them. Bellow seems to side with his heroes. Like them he pays little attention to women as complex creatures. He gives us types—the career woman (Iva and Mary), the pure housewife (Marie or Anna), the wise old woman (Grandma Lausch or Willatale). These types are often strong-willed.

The women live in a world of fathers and sons. Henderson and the other heroes pursue their identity, their masculinity, in relation to other males. This pursuit is always ambivalent. So we find in Bellow's fiction a never-ending, *substantial* embodiment of themes or ideas. All his men are looking for wisdom. They see strangers as holding secrets of power. I have suggested that frequently Bellow does not give us the information we need to understand psychological complexities. Perhaps he cannot face the family history of his characters—remember that we get only hints about Joseph's or Asa's parents—because the history is so "personal." But he should give us more than he does.

Despite these limitations, Bellow's characters are alive—how much do *we* know about our family ties? —because they, at least, realize that other people exist. They touch strangers. They even achieve a kind of greatness, particularly in *Seize the Day*, where Tommy Wilhelm rises above type-casting. This greatness is, as Schlossberg says, "exactly human." It reaffirms the necessary belief that it is our nature to choose freely between good and evil.

4

The Images

Bellow is more interested in "metaphysical" questions than in mere craftsmanship, but he realizes that he can most effectively communicate his concerns through images. These images are not odd or forced. They are "natural"; they provide the "scene" in which his characters live. They make us experience the pains of existence. Although the following discussion is "schematic" or "abstract," I do not mean to suggest that the images are simply manipulated. Bellow feels them as do his characters.

Bellow often uses images of weight to express those "pressures" of existence which disturb his heroes.[1] In *Dangling Man* Iva "supports" Joseph, hoping that she can make life more tolerable for him. But her attempt is futile. Life continues to be a "loathsome burden." This burden is often a kind of "weariness of life"—as Goethe says.

The physical environment is a burden for most of the novel. Winds "buffet" Joseph on his daily walks. He sees the battered chicken on his mother-in-law's sink, and the "raveled" entrails are a dark reminder of his own. He looks outside at the Christmas preparations: "immense wreaths were mounted on buildings in the green, menacing air." Bodies are burdens. Minna's body is "pinched" by Abt when he hypnotizes her; her eyes "flinch" under her lids. Joseph beats Etta after she annoys him—she yields with shrieks to his repeated slaps. The spanking resembles his own childhood haircut that he remembers—that haircut "hurt" his curls. And his grandfather is part of the memory—his head "hangs over his grandson," threatening him, weighing him down. A later incident is also remembered: the drops of blood on a quarreling drunkard's face, drops "falling from his head like the first slow drops of a heavy rain in summer." The present burdens of nature then reassert themselves: fog "hovers" over Joseph; the street lamp "bent over the curb like a woman who cannot turn homeward until she has found the ring or the coin she dropped in the ice and gutter silt." Each person—each new day—is "dark, burdensome." Perhaps the most impressive, "sustained" imagery of weight is in this passage:

> To many in the fascinated crowd the figure of the man on the ground must have been what it was to me—a prevision. Without warning, *down*. A stone, a girder, a bullet flashes against the head, the bone gives like *glass* from a cheap kiln; or a subtler enemy escapes the *bonds of years*, the *blackness comes down*; *we lie, a great weight on our faces, straining toward the last breath which comes like the gritting of gravel under a heavy tread.* [my italics]

The Victim is also full of burdens, pressures, weights. Even the epigraph contains them: the Ifrit's son is slain by stones (from dates) thrown at him. Elena "pressures" Asa into coming to Staten Island. The muggy air presses continually down upon him. These various pressures—of the body, mind, and atmosphere—are found throughout Asa's adventures, not merely in the first two chapters. Here are some more. Allbee appears and threatens him, "crowding" him on the park bench. After his initial appearance, the clouds are "heavily suspended and slow." Under them Asa remembers his burden as a Jew at a party, then in Rudiger's office—no place is free. Although

Asa does "not look as burdened as he [feels]," he must carry his cross.[2] On the ferry he thinks of the laborers in the engine room working the huge thing: "each turn must be like a repeated strain on the hearts and ribs of the wipers there near the keel." In Elena's rooms he sees "hovering" flies, menacing dishes. Her mother, with "the severity of her head pressed back on her shoulders," threatens him. Asa philosophizes about these various pressures: "Oh, there was a smashup somewhere, certainly, a smashup and a tragic one. . . . Something crushing, a real smash." Later "his high, thick chest, [feels] intolerably bound and compressed, and he [lifts] his shoulders in an effort to ease his breathing." But what's the use? He continues to be crushed—like Mary's letter in his hand.

The images are dense in the latter half of the novel. Asa goes to the park and finds there an "overwhelming human closeness and thickness"—millions seem to touch him. Allbee strengthens this feeling when he tells his victim that "the world's a crowded place" even the dead "get buried in layers." His very presence is a "great tiring weight." Asa is "mauled" as children —like Philip or Mickey—are mauled. Perhaps the heaviest weight is found here: "He had the strange feeling that there was not a single part of him on which the whole world did not press with full weight, on his body, on his soul, pushing upward in his breast and downward in his bowels."

Of course, *The Adventures of Augie March* are "lighter" than those of Asa and Joseph because the hero is a *luftmensch*—a man of air. But still there are burdens. Despite the fact that Augie immediately informs us about his "free" style, he does come from Chicago, "that somber city" of crowds, pressure-winds. Can he be less heavy than the physical atmosphere?

Augie is perhaps more interested in the burdens of history—as are Joseph and Asa, who constantly think of the family weighing them down—than the physical environment. He must breathe while other eras—previous greatness—lie on him. Thus we have an image which recurs throughout his adventures; Augie carries Einhorn:

> [I] got him on my back. He used to talk about himself as the Old Man of the Sea riding Sinbad. But there was Aeneas too, who carried his old dad Anchises in the buring of Troy.

As Augie carries Einhorn, Grandma Lausch carries the March family, and Simon later carries his relatives.

Everywhere people bear things. Augie is so much a part of his "dark, burdensome" environment that his language itself is loaded with things—lists of people or heavy objects or feelings. His epic catalogues are really "labored" enumerations: "gift robes and wrappers, venetian mirrors and chateaux-in-the-moonlight tapestries." [3] The people are often in "absolute abasement" to his language as, he tells us, the children were to Elisha's bear or the "cracked-down" Jew was to "divine blows."

We could multiply these images of weight. The bargain department under the sidewalk where Augie thinks people trample him; the "thickened and caked machine-halted silence" felt by Einhorn; the "machine materials that withstand steam, gases, and all inhuman pressure"; the "heavy nourishing air" which doesn't last—all these burden Augie, who screams out: How can I remove the mass of "uniform things?" His question is never answered.

Tommy Wilhelm, the "man of sorrows," tries to lighten his burden by "casting off" his real name—heredity itself. But he cannot do this, as he cannot really get rid of his own "thickness of speech." The "peculiar burden of his existence [lies] upon him like an accretion, a load, a hump. In any moment of quiet, when sheer fatigue prevented him struggling, he was apt to feel this mysterious weight." This mysterious weight produces "suffocation or apoplexy." Even Dr. Adler refuses to carry anyone—including his own son—on his back. Life is enough of a burden already. As Tommy realizes more dramatically: "they ride on me with hoofs and claws." Because he does see his burden eventually, he becomes Christlike. (His father talks about crosses, and the burdens are crosses). But even when he lightens his load in ecstatic crying, the tears convulse him, "bending his stubborn head."

On the first page Henderson has a "pressure in the chest," thinking of the facts of his disorderly life. His entire body is a "great weight." He believes that he can lighten his existential burdens by shifting them, by doing manual labor, but the voice within pressures him. As if "there were strangulation in [his] heart," he clutches the violin, trying to reach his dead father. The weights continue to lie on him.

He sees life in America as *junk*—like the "bottles, lamps, old butter dishes," that he finds in the old woman's cottage. But even in Africa there is junk. The frogs—great, powerful, spotted—lie in the cistern. By blasting them out, Henderson can lift some of the burdens of the Arnewi tribe and his own. However, he destroys the cistern as well as the frogs. The Wariri ruler, Dahfu, lives in a dense atmosphere—witness the "volupté" of the Amazons which "presses" him and Henderson. The rituals themselves are supposed to free humanity from divine weight. That is why Henderson strains to lift Mummah, even though his body has been "loaded" with "vices, like a raft, a barge." He speaks to the idol. " 'Up you go, dearest, no use trying to make yourself heavier; if you weighed twice as much I'd lift you anyway.' " And he does. But he also meets the lion, to see if "man is a creature who cannot stand still under blows." Dahfu doesn't flinch under the lion's weight. Henderson does. Finally he learns to let go, and his own lion qualities come out after being inhibited for such a long time. When Dahfu hunts his father-lion, he must lie above the animal's cage. Suddenly he falls and the animal *stamps* him to death.

Henderson realizes then that the pressures, burdens, and weights of life are never lifted.

Bellow often uses images of deformity or disease to express the painful mortality we bear. His employment of such images is "traditional": Oedipus, Samson, and St. Paul are blind. Bellow joins many ancient writers in asserting that the body itself—"shapeless," clumsy, or crippled—is less beautiful than the will or spirit. It is the necessary "weight" we carry. (For the purpose of this essay I have separated these two images but they are often united, as are all the images I discuss.)

Dangling Man presents the "deterioration" of Joseph. Living in a "narcotic dullness," he is sick like "coughing" Vanaker next door or his "unmanly" father-in-law—but his sickness is of the soul. Still, he sees universal physical deformity: Minna's hypnotized body; the "crooking" vein on Iva's temple; his own "crammed feeling" at his heart; his grandfather's "withered fist"; the street of his childhood where a cripple who taunted his brother and beggars "with sores and deformities" lived; the "cuttings and waste from the body"; the "Parisian cripple" renting out his hump; and Walter Farson's baby with a gag in her mouth. Two illnesses are stressed. Joseph sees a man fall in front of him—a heart attack—and he cannot resist gazing at his "swollen lips," his "helpless tongue." Mrs. Kiefer, the landlady, has a stroke that paralyzes her legs. Her illness dominates his thoughts for a good part of the novel. She drags Joseph along—as does the old woman with a scarred forehead who offers him religious pamphlets. (The latter's face "burns and wastes" under his eyes.) The total effect of these deformities is great; Joseph realizes that the body is crippled, imperfect; only the will can—and should—be strong. But he cannot fully regain his health.

The Victim begins on a note of sickness: Asa finds out that his nephew is bedridden. This illness is repeated throughout the novel. Thus Mr. Beard, Asa's boss, has a "face enlarged by baldness." Elena's eyes are "anxious, altogether too bright and too liquid"; there is a "superfluous energy in her movements." Asa has "unreliable nerves," an occasional tremor. Allbee's "lower jaw slipped to one side, his glum, contemplative eyes filled with a green and leaden color." Asa remembers everyone years ago speaking of "brain fever"—this in reference to his mother's illness. Elena's mother resembles an "ugly old witch."

Why is there so much disease? Asa is preoccupied with disease because it signifies the "freakish" process of living, that process which singles out one disease from one person: "One child in thousands. How did they account for it? Did everyone have it dormant? Could it be heredity? Or, on the other hand, was it even more strange that people, so different, did not have more individual diseases?" Such questions plague him. He sees disease as "metaphysical"—as do *The Magic Mountain, The Rack, Lady Chatterley's Lover,* and *The Idiot.* Perhaps Thomas Mann's remarks help to explain Asa's preoccupation:

> The truth is that life has never been able to do without the morbid, and probably no adage is more inane than the one which says that "only disease can come from the diseased." Life is not prudish, and it is probably safe to say that life prefers creative, genius-bestowing disease a thousand times over to prosaic health; prefers disease, surmounting obstacles proudly on horseback, boldly leaping from peak to peak, to lounging, pedestrian healthfulness. Life is not finical and never thinks of making a moral distinction between health and infirmity. It seizes the bold product of disease, consumes and digests it, and as soon as it is assimilated, it is health.[4]

Surrounded by disease, Asa is forced to seek "healthy" answers to existence—if any exist. Although he never achieves "prosaic health," to use Mann's phrase, he does learn to cope with life as disease and, paradoxically enough, becomes less diseased as a result: "The consciousness of an unremitting daily fight, though still present, was fainter and less troubling. His health was better, and there were changes in his appearance."

In 1949 Bellow published "A Sermon by Doctor Pep," which pursues the subject of disease.[5] The "doctor" leans on a crutch and speaks not of yogurt but of the linkage of disease and health. He suggests that we cannot separate them: "in health we are in the debt of a suffering creation." Although he has only one foot, he values his deformity; it has taught him to walk with a new step, to see life as it really is. He is better than the healthy ones dying of satiety; they keep death too near by "secret care." Pep and the crutch are married!

And the cripples multiply in *The Adventures of Augie March*. Augie lovingly depicts the various deformities of people he knows—he delights in his occult knowledge of disease. Unlike Joseph and Asa, he is not terrified; he remains full of pep.

Remember that we first see the March family discussing new glasses for Mama. Mama has few teeth left, large feet; Grandma Lausch is as "wrinkled as an old paper bag"; Georgie is an idiot with "stiff" feet; even the dog Winnie is "loud-breathing." Augie is somehow healthy, but he suffers from mental turmoil. Their friends are also deformed or diseased. Friedl Coblin has the "impediment of Moses whose hand the watching angel guided to the coal." Anna Coblin "butchered on herself with pains and fears"; she is likened to a martyr with a "mangled head." Coblin's eyes blink "just about to point of caricature." Mama March gets sick; she lies "dumbly" in bed. Einhorn is a cripple whose hands function weakly; he resembles the deformed Hephaestus, who made "ingenious machines"—a god of "cranks, chains, and metal parts." The world itself becomes for Augie a place of "special disfigurement." Later he repeats this comment when he looks at the West Side station:

> It was very dark. It was spoiled, diseased, sore and running. And as the mis-minted and wrong-struck figures and faces stooped, shambled, strode, gazed, dreaded, surrendered, didn't care . . . You wondered that all was stuff that was born human and shaped human, and over the indiscriminateness and lack of choice.

No wonder that love itself is a "peculiarity."

Tommy Wilhelm also lives in a world of "freaks." When he greets Rubin, he notices the man's "poor" eyes. The other man gazes at him, making him self-conscious. Then Tommy looks at himself in the mirror, thinking that he is sick: "A wide wrinkle like a comprehensive bracket sign was written upon his forehead, the point between his brows, and there were patches of brown on his dark blond skin." He calls himself a "fair-haired hippopotamus!" Dr. Adler, on the other hand, takes good care of his body, but this, in itself, is a kind of sickness; as Tommy realizes, such "health" is diseased. Mr. Perls walks with a heavy cane; he has "dyed hair and fish teeth." Dr. Tamkin is deformed: "his bones were peculiarly formed as though twisted twice where the ordinary human was turned only once, and his shoulders rose in two pagoda-like points." His eyes are full of "strange lines." He thinks the world is a hospital—businessmen "spread the plague." Mr. Rappaport is blind; he has to be led across the street by Tommy. Like Augie March, our hero has a vision of *sick humanity*. In the subway tunnel he sees the "haste, heat, and darkness which disfigure and make freaks and fragments of nose and eyes and teeth." Right here he loves the "lurid-looking people." Though he gets "all choked-up" later, he heals himself—that is, he sees his disease, and realizes there is no *cure*.

In *Henderson the Rain King* the underlying image becomes "exaggerated," until it is the basis of philosophical discussion. Again Bellow suggests the symbolic nature of disease; *"description" is idea.* Like all of Bellow's heroes, Eugene Henderson is deformed. Just look at him: "At birth I weighed fourteen pounds, and it was a tough delivery. Then I grew up. Six feet four inches tall. Two hundred and thirty pounds. An enormous head, rugged, with hair like Persian lambs' fur." And a "great nose." He is somewhat "loony," smashing bottles, wallowing in mud. Everyone he knows suffers from disease or deformity. Lily wears a bridge—like Henderson; she is nearly six feet tall; and she has ugly dyed hair. (But she is "beautiful" for her husband.) The dead neighbor, Miss Lenox, has a "small, toothless face." In Africa Henderson learns the significance of disease. His "physical discrepancies" are discussed by Willatale and then by Dahfu. Willatale herself—toothless, the "flesh of her arm overlapping her elbow"—is not particularly beautiful. She appreciates the peculiarities of Henderson, finding in his physical appearance a great longing for spiritual elevation. When she agrees that he should study medicine—note how the doctor-figure reappears —he is happy, so happy that his gums itch. She *and* he know that happiness is always tinged with illness. *Humanity is never "healthy"*:

> Oh, it's miserable to be human. You get such queer diseases. Just because you're human and for no other reason. Before you know it, as the years go by, you're just like other people you have seen, with all those peculiar human ailments.

Humanity is a "regular bargain basement of deformities."

Dahfu, a "medicine man," can help cure Henderson. His conversation circles about notions of health: Man is an artist; his principal work of art is the body. "Disease is a speech of the psyche." Because no one is ever completely free—"divine"—he is always sick, developing bodily symptoms. It seems that Dahfu has read Thomas Mann, Nietzsche, and Dostoyevsky as well as Wilhelm Reich.

Does Henderson ever become healthy? No, if we mean that he is free of the "body-speech" of the psyche. He continues to endure his pain. Occasionally he feels well—cured for an instant—as in the end of the novel. The following passage sums up the significance of disease in all of Bellow's novels; it suggests that disease is the spirit talking poorly, health just the opposite.

> I told the kid, "Inhale. Your face is too white from your orphan's troubles. Breathe in this air, kid, and get a little color." I held him close to my chest. He didn't seem to be afraid that I would fall with him. While to me he was like medicine applied, and the air too; it also was a remedy.

Humanity should seek the *remedy* of love.

One image which is less important than weight or deformity is cannibalism. Bellow associates cannibalism with our "diseased" condition; people *consume* each other as the germ consumes the body.

Dangling Man gives us the following examples: Joseph, in talking about his plight, says: "I am deteriorating, storing bitterness and spite which eat like acids at my endowment of generosity and good will." He is "fed up." When he goes to the Almstadts, he describes in details the consumed chicken, "its yellow claws rigid, its head bent as though to examine its entrails which raveled over the sopping drain board." He later describes his grandfather's head "devouring" him. History itself consumes us, joining our own cannibalistic feasts. So do our idealizations: they "consume us like parasites"; yet we invite such parasites, "as if we were eager to be drained and eaten." Joseph, depleted by the parasites around and within him, remains "hungry," even after eating a large dinner, a whole package of caramels, and a bag of mints.

One way of regarding *The Victim* is seeing Allbee and Asa as parasite and host (or vice versa). Even before we recognize this hideous relationship, Bellow gives us references to food. Asa Leventhal is "hungry" after he visits Elena; his hunger is, in a way, an outward sign of psychological needs. He "satisfies" his hunger with a good meal; "his mood gradually improved." But something makes him feel empty again; he drinks the milk in the refrigerator. Asa is being consumed, but he doesn't know the cause. After Allbee begins to taunt him, we get vicious consumption: Asa thinks of "little burning worms that seemed to eat up rather than give light"; he sees Allbee as a parasite; he begins to see that hideous things, "cannibalistic things," exist in the world. In a complete vision he sees humanity in terms of food—an egg: "We were . . . running as if in an egg race with the egg in a spoon. And sometimes we were fed up with the egg, sick of it." He continues to be hungry—but unable to "swallow another bite."

The imagery of food—of starvation and parasitism—strongly asserts itself in Dr. Pep's sermon: Humanity "kills and devours"; "death inhibits the bite, it poisons each mouthful"; we "turn our appetite on ourselves." But Dr. Pep suggests that there is always hunger which must be satisfied. Even divine food is devoured: "Or turn your thoughts to eucharistic wine and wafers. 'You shall eat my body and drink my blood.'" Jesus and the hamburger are related; both are needed to satisfy our hunger—we consume as we love. This "secret of health and eating," Dr. Pep tells us, is found in a Paschal lamb, a fish, the holy wafer. "Is there any real love short of eating?" Although the doctor realizes that our hunger—base, "other directed"—cannot be completely satisfied, he hopes that it forces us to eat more substantial food—divinity itself.

This mad sermon resembles an essay written by Bellow's close friend, Isaac Rosenfeld, on Jewish taboos. The essay, entitled "Adam and Eve on Delancey

Street," stresses the symbolic nature of food. Here are some fascinating passages which throw some light on the doctor's concern:

> The simple act of eating has become for us the Jews a complicated ceremonial, from the preparatory phases of ritual slaughter, through *milchigs* and *fleishigs*, kosher and *treif*, to benedictions and postprandial prayers. It is for such reasons, among others, that the Jewish religion enjoys the reputation of being one of the most wordly and immanent, one of the most closely connected with daily life. What Sacred Communion is to Catholics, the everyday mealtime is to Orthodox Jews.[6]
>
> There is great charm in a religion that can thus coalesced along the two lines of sacred and secular without any apparent break; it avoids the usual dualism, the conflict in belief or realm against realm.[7]

Dr. Pep's advice also avoids the "usual dualism"; in fact, he is perhaps a healthier individual than the Jew who, according to Rosenfeld, represses his needs by submitting to food taboos.

Although Augie March doesn't preach any sermon about cannibalism, parasitism, or the true consumption of food, he is disgusted—and fascinated!—by the immense meals Anna Coblin prepares. Eating becomes a wholly monstrous activity, "self-centered," materialistic, and lacking any spiritual meaning. The Coblins—and most of Augie's friends and relatives—are cannibals; they devour people as they do their luxurious meals. They are "human barbecuers." In his discussion of the "axial lines of life," Augie mentions Osiris, the god torn apart by his followers. Osiris is an ideal because the "devoured" god is somehow regenerated. Is Augie?

Food is emphasized in *Seize the Day*. When Tommy decides to have Coca-Cola with his breakfast, Mr. Perls and Dr. Adler are shocked. Eating is as unbalanced as his whole life. As he devours himself with guilt, so he eats and eats: "He did not hurry but kept putting food on his plate until he had gone through the muffins and his father's strawberries." Tommy is always hungry, more so than Asa. So is Dr. Tamkin, who even manages to devour food after the stock fluctuations. Of course, he is a parasite—he uses the word himself to describe the pretender soul: "Biologically, the pretender soul takes away the energy of the true soul and makes it feeble, like a parasite." He feeds upon Tommy; that is why our hero is always hungry. Later Tommy refers to his environment as food, wanting to breathe, once again, the "sugar of the pure morning." But he eats unsatisfying Coca-Cola and pills.

Henderson, like Tommy, is "hungry" for some meaning; his *I want! I want!* is an "infant's" cry for food. Wherever he turns, he sees parasitism or cannibalism. He remembers the octopus in the aquarium: "the creature seemed also to look at me and press its soft head to the glass." Does the creature—a symbol of death?—want to eat him? In Africa the Arnewi cows are "dying of thirst"; the frogs feed upon them by polluting their water. Henderson is so conscious of food that he feels sorry for the nursing infants who are taken away from their mothers' breasts (the mothers, by showing them to him, disrupt their meal). (Once, he remembers, he wanted to feed a baby seal, but one of the beachcombers objected, saying that if he fed the seal it would "encourage the creature to be a parasite on the beach.") Is there any proper food in life?

Henderson learns that love can transform food. Dahfu shows him that the lion will not devour him, although lions hunger for flesh. But the lesson is forgotten after Dahfu is consumed by his false lion-father. Parasitism remains. So does Henderson's spiritual appetite.

The previous images suggest that life is dangerous, ugly, and heavy. Thus Bellow's characters consider themselves imprisoned. In *Dangling Man* Joseph is locked in his room, rarely leaving it. The boarding house, itself, is a prison for the inhabitants—for him, Vanaker, and the landlady. The mental environment is also a prison: Joseph tries to keep himself "intact," shut-up, so that his feelings will not overly upset him; Minna is rigid, entrapped by Morris' hypnosis. People in general, Joseph says, are no longer impenetrable. Even if they want to remain alone in their "mental rooms," they cannot: someone knocks. The "craters of the spirit" are visible. (Does the emphasis on craters link our hero to the biblical Joseph who finds himself in several pits?) People constitute an "empire of ice boxes."

Three extended descriptions reveal the underlying claustrophobia of the novel. At one point we learn this from Joseph:

> I, in this room, separate, alienated, distrustful, find in my purpose not an open world, but a closed, hopeless jail. My perspectives end in the walls. Nothing of the future comes to me. Only the past, in its shabbiness and innocence. Some men seem to know exactly where their opportunities lie; they break prisons and cross whole Siberias to pursue them. One room holds me.

When he visits his childhood room, he discovers that this "great good place"—to use Henry James' phrase—is also a kind of prison from which he never escapes. "Home" does not really exist—only an ambiguous prison.

> The room, delusively, dwindled and became a tiny square, swiftly drawn back, myself and all the objects in its growing smaller. This was not a mere visual trick. I understand it to be a revelation of the ephemeral agreements by which we live and pace ourselves.

The third passage occurs in one of his many nightmares: Joseph finds himself in a "low chamber" with rows of large cribs in which corpses are lying. The corpses look "remarkably infantile." He likens the long room to the rooms in the Industrial Museum—to the terrors of Gehenna his father once conjured for him. The nightmare not only presents the "tomb" of his present existence—it suggests that Joseph is in Hell. There is "no exit" for him.

Tombs, prisons, rigid confinement—all these reappear in *The Victim*. We first see Asa trying to leave the subway car; he barely squeezes through the "black door of the ancient car," uttering curses as he does. But he will not gain freedom—his own mind is a "box" which holds ambivalent attitudes. He continually sees prison around him—he imagines the men locked in the engine room aboard the ferry, their naked, oily bodies; he feels the press of crowds in the park; and the closeness of his own apartment (he leaves "the doors in the flat standing open; it made him feel easier.") This claustrophobia becomes "metaphysical": "You couldn't find a place in your feelings for everyone or give at every touch like a swinging door the same for everyone with people going in and out as they pleased. On the other hand, if you shut yourself up, not wanting to be bothered, then you were like a bear in a winter hole." Life offers a swinging door or a locked room, but both choices are deceptive. The images continue: the "cashier's dazzling cage" in the restaurant; Asa's clasped hands "which would require great effort" to open; Allbee's claim that Jews keep "their spirit under lock and key"; the locked gate of the railroad station in Asa's dream; Allbee's statement that the world's an "overcrowded place"; and the story of the man on the subway tracks, "pinned" against the wall. Responding to so many images, Asa resembles the "man in a mine who could smell smoke and feel heat but never see the flames."

Surprisingly enough, *The Adventures of Augie March* contains many prisons—we wonder if Augie can avoid them more successfully than Asa or Joseph. On the first page he tells us that he will knock at the door of life—"sometimes an innocent knock, sometimes a not so innocent." He shuns confinement—

there are open doors! But Augie finds that there are many doors which remain closed, even after he knocks. Several "institutions" are significant in this respect: George's "dummy-room" at the "penal-looking school" which has the "great gloom inside of clinks the world over"; the Home to which George is sent—that home with "wired windows, dog-proof cyclone fence, asphalt yard, great gloom"; the home for the blind where Mama is sent; Grandma Lausch's institution; and the university with the old-world-imitated walls. Perhaps the very existence of such prisons of the spirit compel Augie to picture life a bit differently toward the end of the novel when he says: "we left what company we were in and went privately to take a few falls with our select antagonist, in his secret room, like inside a mountain or down in a huge root-cellar." Everyone has a secret room where his furies lie —including larky Augie. No matter what preparations for life he finally makes, a man is always within "the walls of his being. And all high conversation would take place within the walls of his being. And all achievement would stay within those walls."

Tommy Wilhelm's hotel is the perfect setting for confinement—the drapes in the lobby keep out the sun; after breakfast the old guests sit down in the lobby and stay there the whole day. But the lobby is not his only prison. Tommy remembers the line of poetry: "Sunk though he be beneath the wat'ry floor" because he himself is in a pit. Later he sees the moth trapped on the window pane; he thinks of the lack of space for his car. If only he can find a way out! But the novel insists on more entrapment, showing him that there is really no exit. Tommy "recognizes" death, the "end of all distractions," and of wrong tied tight within his chest, knowing he cannot stay in the same room with his father. New York City is a great hell; the "waters of the earth" are going to roll over him.

Slowly Tommy adjusts to the walls of his being. The imagery shows us his transformation: in the dark subway tunnel he blazes with love for the others—the tunnel, as hellish as it appears, holds a possibility of expansive love. So does the funeral parlor, another dark room. Like the corpse in the coffin, Tommy "recognizes" death, the "end of all distractions," and cries. His crying sinks deeper than his imprisoned being—so deep that it shows him an opening at the bottom. There is an exit!

Some of the short stories contain the same kind of images. Rogin in "A Father-to-Be" is trapped in the "water-filled hollow" of the sink; he submits to his "mother's" shampooing. Bellow implies the sink is a kind of womb; the image captures Rogin's oedipal plight. In "Looking for Mr. Green," the messenger, Grebe, sees many houses from which he is barred; all of them are old and ugly. Chicago itself is a "giant raw place," a "layer of ruins." Mr. Green, if he exists, doesn't live in any great, good place. The Wrecker, of course, realizes that he must destroy the prison of conventional marriage—imagistically, he wrecks his apartment, informing the onlookers: "the old must go down." He wants to "tear out the laths and get behind all the swellings"—to see new spaces.

In "Leaving the Yellow House," which appeared in the January, 1958 issue of *Esquire*, we again find the prison. Old Hattie does not want to leave her yellow house—it is all she has. But she and her neighbors understand that with her broken limbs, she cannot really take care of it. The house is "two-sided": it is the great, good place and prison. Perhaps Bellow suggests that before we can refashion dark prisons, we must accept them. Only then can imprisonment be "cozy." This is why Hattie wills the yellow house to herself.

> She resumed her letter of instructions to lawyer Claiborne; "Upon the following terms," she wrote a second time. "Because I have suffered much. Because I have only lately received what I have to give away. I can't bear it." The drunken blood was soaring to her

head. But her hand was clear enough. She wrote, "It is too soon! Too soon! Because I do not find it in my heart to care for anyone as I would wish. Being cast off and lonely, and doing no harm where I am. Why should it be? This breaks my heart. In addition to everything else, why must I worry about this, which I must leave? I am tormented out of my mind. Even though by my own fault I have put myself into this position. And am not ready to give up on this. No, not yet. And so I'll tell you what, I leave this property, land, house, garden and water rights to Hattie Simmons Waggoner. Me!"

Henderson resembles Augie and the Wrecker in trying to destroy all prisons. His expensive house is unpleasant; even his books are sinister containers of money. The cage in the aquarium more completely signifies entrapment. There an octopus presses its soft head to the glass—the creature is death itself. Henderson does not want to be locked in by money or biological factors; he wants to be in open space. But wherever he turns in America—that giant cage!—he sees more prisons: his father shut up in a room; the dead woman in the rubbish-filled cottage. Africa is not really different: the frogs lie in the cistern, contaminating the water. When Henderson wrecks the cistern, he doesn't see any hope for "proper shelter." And he is confined in an actual prison by the Wariri—in the room is a corpse which reminds him of the dead old woman, the octopus, his father. What if he himself is thrown into a pit? Henderson wonders. The rooms "increase." Dahfu, the Wariri ruler, lives in a luxurious palace which is actually a prison guarded by amazons. He suggests to the American that he is trapped by his tribal commitments; the only way he can "travel" is by reflection. Later both of them enter the dark tunnel where the lion is imprisoned; this reminds Henderson of the octopus' tank, suggesting death. Still afraid that there isn't any exit, he learns to adjust to prisons. He even accepts the tunnel. Unfortunately, he is trapped once more. When Dahfu falls into the lion's cage, meeting his death, Henderson realizes that mere acceptance of confinement will not *end* it—life is always a cage: "*my life and deeds were a prison.*" Although we last see him in the open—"leaping, leaping, pounding"—we realize that this is an interlude before another entrapment. Africa has taught him that any continent is a prison: one never leaves it.

Another crucial image in Bellow's fiction is the beast. Not only are his characters pressed, trapped, devoured, or deformed—they are turned into animals. The image asserts itself in the early fiction, but it is fully developed later. In *Dangling Man* we find several beasts: the "werewolf," Vanaker, a "queer, annoying creature" paces in the hallways and his room; the "nasty, brutish, short" quotation from Hobbes; the idea that "as animals instinctively sought salt or lime, we, too, flew together" at high occasions to destroy one another. Joseph is convinced that the line between bestiality and humanity is very thin at times; *existence is a jungle.* Although we easily accustom ourselves to slaughter, he thinks, we are silly enough to take better care of pets than our neighbors. Even the physical environment is bestial—fog and rain make the street "an imagined swamp where death waited in the thickened water, his lizard jaws open." No wonder that the "heart, like a toad, exudes its fear with a repulsive puff." Perhaps, Joseph thinks, the Egyptians were right in making one of their gods a cat—"only a cat's eye could see into the interior darkness" without fear and trembling.

"The notions of inherent baseness, of human nature sharing the bestiality of nature itself" are in *The Victim*; Asa like "each of Bellow's heroes finds the beast within." [8] Early in the novel the image asserts itself. Asa calls Mr. Beard a "God-damned fish" after the employer starts to reprimand him. At home he thinks of mice darting along the walls. But the mice and fish are not so "full-bodied" as the later beasts. Asa begins to see animals everywhere—aboard the ferry he sees the yellow light on the water, which he compares to

> the slit of the eye of a wild animal, say a lion, something inhuman that didn't care about anything human and yet was implanted in every human being too, one speck of it, and formed a part of him that responded to the heat and glare, exhausting as these were, or even to freezing, salty things, harsh things, all things difficult to stand.

Nature itself is wild; is it any wonder that humanity reflects it? Asa's vision is not very comforting. Neither is his description of the "fly hovering below the tarnish and heat" of Elena's ceiling, or the "immense moths" filled with holes.

After Allbee enters, the images increase: we have many different creatures. The intruder seems "no more human" to Asa than a "fish or crab or any fleshy thing in the water." While he thinks this, he imagines that a mouse scurries past. Later Asa wants to be "like a bear in a winter hole," hiding from Allbee and the whole freakish process of living. The most sustained beast-description is found in the zoo incident. When he and Philip visit the zoo on their outing, Asa loses his sense of the "usual," seeing only the bars and cages, the dust and manure, the "ferocity of animal life"—so conscious of the animals is he that he immediately thinks of Allbee as a beast. Afterwards he reveals his feelings to his tyrant: "Everyday I see new twists. . . . They say you go to the zoo to see yourself in the animals. There aren't enough animals in the world to see ourselves in. There would have to be a million new feathers and tails. There's no end to the twists." Allbee counters by saying: You look like Caliban! The vision of bestial humanity becomes a vision

of the bestial universe—possibilities, conditions, potentialities—all represented by the word "if"—"swing
us around by the ears like rabbits."

The beasts appear in "A Sermon by Doctor Pep."
Again this sermon points the way to new directions;
here our animal-likeness is "accepted," even loved.
Unlike Joseph and Asa, Dr. Pep realizes that to be
human is to be animalistic—there is no way out—but
the animalistic qualities are often "good," keeping us
in touch with nature, not the mechanized city. Once
we accept the delightful chirping of birds, we must
also accept ferocious lions. Birds, lions, human beings
—all creatures are *alive*. Consequently, Dr. Pep embraces the butterflies in the air, his own "dog-white
hair," the lamb of Christianity, the "indiscriminate
feasting sow," the "blood of steers," his fur-lined coat,
the Lincoln Park Zoo as a favorite home—all these
things "are images of spirit, icons, symbols, versions
and formations."

Augie March is also at home with the beasts. Like
the monkeys who see no evil, speak no evil, hear no
evil, he accepts the bestiality around him, loving the
"fighting nature of birds and worms" which Grandma
Lausch has. Zeus, who appears on earth as an animal,
symbolizes for him the bond of gods and beasts. The
wonder of human beings is that they can be animalistic *and* godlike—that is, "exactly human." Of course,
the bestial part of us is sometimes unpleasant—greedy,
fearful—but we must be beavers ("I suffered like a
beaver") or wolves (pacing in "the pit of the zoo" as
Einhorn does during his deals) before we can show
"stubborn animal spirit." The "male piercingness,
sharpness, knotted hard muscle" of Chanticleer is
achieved after the disturbed beauty of nightingales,
Caligula, Thea's eagle, is viewed in two different ways
by Augie. The eagle is brutish, sharp, fierce—but it is
also an object of love (Caligula is less bestial than his
trainer, Thea Fenchel). The eagle—like all the beasts
—is dangerous and pathetic. It is almost human in its

mixture. Thus Augie can later say about his soul, it's like other souls, as "one lion is pretty nearly all the lions." The soul and the lion—the image suggests their marriage.

Bellow suggests that one needs courage to accept the bestial soul. Tommy Wilhelm, like the weak Asa or Joseph, perceives only the threat or absurdity of animal-likeness, not "stubborn animal spirit." He sees himself as a "fair-haired hippopotamus"; Maurice Venice as a sloppy ox (there is also something "fishy" about the agent); his own bearlike posture; Mr. Perls as a "damn frazzle-faced herring with his dyed hair and fish teeth." The beasts here are "silly" (like herrings), not courageous (like lions). Because Bellow uses the imagery in a different way, he creates a *different zoo* in *Seize the Day*. It is too easy to say that he simply repeats the same kind of image; his beasts are carefully selected. When Tommy describes his "sheep dog," for example, he sees himself as the animal—gentle, friendly, but easily misled. When he looks closely at Dr. Tamkin, he sees a bird of prey with "hypnotic power" in his eyes, and "claw-like" nails. He can easily accept the charlatan's story about the lonely person "howling from his window like a wolf." Tommy's most extended description of beasts is this one: "On the road, he frequently passed chicken farms. Those, big, rambling wooden lights burned all night in them to cheat the poor hens into laying. Then the slaughter." He sees himself, finally, as a "poor hen," devoured by the "claw-like" world.

Many critics have discussed the beasts in *Henderson the Rain King*. Daniel Hughes writes:

> Daniel's remark to Nebuchadnezzar, referred to throughout the novel, gives us the clue: "They shall drive thee from among men and thy dwelling shall be with beasts of the fields." This reduction (or exaltation) to the animal defines Henderson's characteristic experience. He begins as a breeder of pigs and returns with a lion cub; in between he suffers degradation in

faintly parodic imitation of Lear, who is also forced to the animal and undergoes an actual and symbolic stripping.[9]

Henderson has many confrontations with beasts, as Mr. Hughes indicates; these affirm the bond between animal and human being. Here the beasts are not so "silly" as the ones in *Seize the Day*: they are stubborn, fierce, and strong. At the end of the novel Henderson profits from his savage encounters (especially with the lions), understanding that he cannot escape from his "heart of darkness." Here are Mr. Hughes words:

> As with any resonant poetic symbol, no linear meaning can be attributed to the lion and lion-king of this novel. Indeed, this is a symbol, wholly integrated with Henderson's quest, thus forming an interesting contrast with the eagle-ritual that Augie March undergoes in a partly real, partly symbolic Mexico. . . . The lion kept under the throne by Dahfu is precisely what Henderson is not, something external, powerful, real. For all his boasting about reality, Henderson must undergo a savage encounter with something entirely foreign, and from this discover reality in himself.[10]

By crouching on all fours, imitating the lion, Henderson fulfills Daniel's prophecy. But he has one more confrontation—this time with Dahfu's lion-father, Gmilo (it turns out to be another lion). This new lion —like the octopus in the cage—symbolizes death; it can never be completely mastered. The animal images in *Henderson the Rain King* are "deep"; they are more thoroughly developed than the few in *Dangling Man*, showing us again Bellow's consistent advancement.

Because Bellow's characters feel trapped, pressured, and even devoured by the environment (and themselves), they want, at least consciously, to move. They *search* for answers to their predicaments. But their movements are usually erratic, circular, violent, or nonpurposeful.

Look at *Dangling Man*. Although Joseph is "imprisoned," he also sees himself as "dangling"—he insists that he "shall have to be cut down," before he can estimate the damage his "swinging" has caused him. There are other "useless" movements: Vanaker's mad pacing; Joseph's fearful walks—these are contrasted to the purposeful "rocketing" of Tad to Africa or regular seasonal change, which Joseph, quoting Goethe, would like to emulate. In this opposition of useless and purposeful movement, the useless movement asserts itself more strongly: fierce winds or rain; the blood-sopping draining board on which the chicken lies; the "grinding" movement of Christmas shoppers; the violent gestures of Joseph as he confronts Burns; the "hacking" of humanity; the graceless flying together of the bestial party guests; Joseph's mean spanking of Etta; his traumatic, early hair-*cut*—all these movements show us that *existence moves without grace*. At several points Joseph philosophizes in similar imagery. He tells us "there is a storm and hate and wounding rain out of us." The "hemispheric blackness" chatters, perhaps answering the human storm. When he tries to seek new directions, go to different places, he sees a man fall violently or a boy thrust a toy gun at him. "Who can be the earnest huntsman of himself when he knows he is in turn a quarry?" All his questions produce this vision: "my mind flapping like a rag on a clothesline in a cold wind."

The Victim uses an epigraph from DeQuincey's *The Pains of Opium*: "Now it was that upon the rocking waters of the ocean the human face began to reveal itself." Existence in a surging ocean. Immediately we are ready for the novel itself. New York "seems to have moved from its place"—this unbalanced, crazy movement is juxtaposed to the "spiritual elevation" of the lights climbing "upward endlessly

into the heat of the sky." Which of the two movements will win? Of course, there is no real contest, as
we can tell from other images on the same page. Asa
jumps up, struggles with the sliding subway door and
squeezes through it. Other frenetic movements follow: Mr. Beard's hand trembles; Asa pushes his arm
violently through his coat-sleeve; Elena has "superfluous energy" in her movements; Mary runs without
grace (in Asa's memory).

Because Asa senses unconsciously the wasted movement (around and within him), he thinks in terms of
cessation of movement or "transfer." The latter is
evident in the many train references: not only does he
struggle with the subway door at the beginning of the
novel—he returns to the image in a "philosophical"
way. He dreams about missing "the right train," after
running desperately to catch it. When he talks to
Allbee, the tyrant claims that all people are traveling
in the wrong train, headed in an obscure direction—
driven by what? After many years the two victims,
now successful, see each other and start talking about
trains. Allbee says: "I've made my peace with things as
they are. I've gotten off the pony—you remember, I
said that to you once? I'm on the train." To which Asa
asks: "A conductor?" Allbee responds: "I'm just a
passenger." *There is no transfer: we remain passen-
gers, not even knowing who runs things.*

And the universal movement is violent, as more
images tell us. "Now it's all blind movement, vast
movement, and the individual is shuttled back and
forth." Sometimes there's a "smashup." Or we "go in
all directions without any limit." Asa, "like everyone
else, [is] carried on currents, this way and that. The
currents had taken a new twist, and he was being
hurried, hurried." There is great "dizziness" in being
human.

Both *Dangling Man* and *The Victim* are "closed"
novels—the various images of movement are under the
surface; they burst forth at important times to de-

scribe "blind, erratic" motives (human or divine). In *The Adventures of Augie March* Bellow gives us what he himself has called "catch-as-catch-can pica-resque."[11] Here the novel itself is "open," in motion: Augie continually travels from one place to another, seeking meta-physical—or real—answers to his questions. The question is: Are Augie's movements purposeful? Or are they as erratic as Asa's? Again there is no simple reply because Bellow constantly juxtaposes useless and purposeful movement, suggesting that life holds both. But he does indicate that Augie is a more "successful" traveler than his earlier heroes.

Within the big movements of this novel, there are smaller ones. Let us look closely at these. In the first chapter Grandma Lausch instructs Augie and others how to go on their mission to the Charities office—*how to travel*. Although he listens to her instructions, we can see already that he is a solitary traveler, seeing his own sights in his own way. His style of movement is reflected—or captured—in his narration. When he tells us that "sometimes we were chased, stoned, bitten and beat up for Christ-killers" we note that his breathless pace is "larky and boisterous," even though he describes painful movement. He tells us often depressing things "on the run." The vital phrases violate —render impotent—useless or cruel movement. They incarnate "progressive," never-ending voyages.

But if we stop long enough to observe the kind of movement Augie "skips over" we find the blind process of *Dangling Man*: the "snipping, cooing hubbub of paper-chain making" in Georgie's school; the sly, often criminal movements of young Augie; the "dizzy watchfulness" of Mama; the "angry giddiness" of Grandma Lausch, her "human enterprise sinking and discharging blindly from a depth"; the crippled, lurching gestures of Einhorn; and the destroying fire in this cripple's house. These movements are "countless disks," circles—not straight lines. These disturb Augie: can he continue on his larky way, aware as he is of erratic movement and dark prisons? He puts the problem this way:

> It was not only for me that being moored wasn't permitted; there was general motion, as of people driven from angles and corners into the open, by places being valueless and inhospitable to them. In the example of the Son of Man having no place to lay His head; or belonging to the world in general . . . I, with my can of paint, no more than others. And once I was underway, street cars weren't sufficient, nor Chicago large enough to hold me.

Yes, he does keep moving, but he gradually begins to recognize that in "the free spinning of the world," breaking out of the small circle is not always completely successful. Out of one circle, he sees others: "Around some people the space is their space, and when you want to approach them it has to be across their territory." It is not that easy to bound "the exploding oceans of universal space." The best one can hope for, according to Augie, is that he become aware of the "axial lines of life, with respect to which you must be straight or else your existence is merely clownery, hiding tragedy." Augie tries, if not to be straight in his movements, to be aware of the circular experiences of the race—the cyclical return of greatness. So we leave him still a traveler, a Columbus: "Why, I'm a sort of Columbus of those near-at-hand and believe you can come to them in this immediate *terra incognita* that spreads out in every gaze." Will he discover America or be shipwrecked? The question is open—like his crisscrossing, happy voyages.

Seize the Day has many movements which are, for the most part, violent, erratic, or useless. Tommy Wilhelm "sinks" throughout his adventures, although he longs to climb upward—when we first see him in the elevator, he sinks and sinks, and after the door opens, he sees the dark, uneven carpet "billow" toward him. Sinking, drowning—these images are contrasted to the bird that he sees beating its wings. Although we have two different kinds of movement, the "bad" will pre-dominate. Thus Tommy's spirits are low; he remem-bers "sunk though he be beneath the watr'y floor"; he thinks of Los Angeles containing "all the loose ob-jects" in the country that slide down there; he swal-lows hard at the Coke bottle; and he fears the *drop* in lard on the stock exchange. These images are not all; Tommy has to contend with violent movement as well as sinking. He thinks of constantly running out to move his car, gesturing wildly while driving, "rolling his blood-shot eyes barbarously," the wrenching of the cemetery bench by vandals, and kicking his bed to pieces. No wonder he needs tranquilizers! But even these cannot *steady* him; he continues to sink or move wildly. His self-control was going out like "a ball in the surf, washed beyond reach." He wants to stop going by "fits and starts and [falling] upon the thorns of life." He doesn't want to be drowned by the money-flow, wanting only to "march in a straight line." Dr. Tamkin's poem contains the images: it suggests that "Everyman" should stop "skimming" the earth's surface and, instead, remain at the foot of Mt. Seren-ity; climbing is dangerous. Tommy is so confused by the poem that he almost foams at the mouth, believ-ing in effect, that the "waters of the earth are going to roll over [him]." After the stock exchange fluctuates madly, he runs to Tamkin's apartment and discovers that the charlatan has fled. Then he joins the pushing crowds and is carried into the chapel. Here the slow, steady movement captures him so much that he sinks into "the final thought"—like the corpse. (Again sink-ing—with a difference: one must sink in order to rise!) The epiphany of Tommy reasserts the images I have been tracing. He writhes with tears, sinking "deeper than sorrow," toward his heart's ultimate needs.

The short stories also contain movement. In "A Father-to-Be" Rogin rides in the subway (the road of life?), enjoying the trip at first. However, the peaceful journey stimulates his mind in unpleasant ways, mak-

ing him think of time as a destructive current: "The
life force occupied each of us in turn in its progress
towards its own fulfillment, trampling on our individual humanity." (He resembles Asa and Allbee in this
thought.) Is there any way to stop the inhuman flow?
Is there any way to shape movement? Rogin finds one
answer in the "green and foaming" fluid in the sink,
but he has simply submitted to Joan's current. In
"Looking for Mr. Green," the messenger, George
Grebe, regards himself as a hunter (like Augie?), seeking the answer to reality in the form of Mr. Green.
But he finds that his quest is painful, not very successful, because he is an outsider. Climbing, walking
through doors, pacing, and running—finally he sees
Miss (or Mrs.) Green and he achieves his goal. Or so
he thinks. Has he shaped his quest or has he been
carried along? The same question applies to Clarence
Feiler, who hunts for Gonzaga manuscripts. "Fanati-
cally" searching out relatives and friends of the dead
poet, he seems to know where he is going. The imagery tells a different—more correct—story. We have
such images as the following: "Holes are torn in the
ocean bottom. The cold water rushes in and cools the
core of the earth." Clarence thinks of the "pouring
rain-cloud" (produced by atomic explosions?). The
various references to earth-*shaking* bombs underlies
our hero's reckless search: he is drowned—comically,
of course—by the system's mad currents. It is appropriate that after he learns this, "the heavens [seem] to
split; a rain [begins] to fall, heavy and sudden, boiling
on the wide plain."

Now we are ready for the movement in *Henderson
the Rain King*. Like Augie, Clarence, and the other
voyagers, our hero is searching for reality. The question is: Is his hunt successful? The imagery offers clues
to the meaning of the novel. It suggests that reality is
erratic *and* orderly, wild *and* peaceful, high *and* low. It
is mixed movement—this is the answer Augie accepts
as do Asa and Allbee at the end of *The Victim*.

The novel begins with a "disorderly rush" as Henderson thinks of his experiences—this rush turns into chaos. He is pictured as shaking out books (to find his father's money), falling off a tractor, and then running over himself, crawling with his pigs, and erratically playing the violin. Henderson decides, imagistically, to correct the rush by taking a trip, *ordering his movement*. Africa, the dark continent, will be chaos or heaven to him. (He is unaware that it is both.) In his airplane he feels at home—"dreaming down at the clouds." But the graceful movement soon ends. In Africa Henderson again sees violent movement: he wrestles with Itelo, falling to the ground; he thinks then that his "spirit's sleep" *bursts*; he blasts the cistern. However, during these bursts of chaotic movement, he dreams again of pink light which makes him "fly" over the white points of the sea at ten thousand feet; he hears Willatale affirm his belief that "the earth is a huge ball which nothing holds up in space except its own motion and magnetism and we conscious things who occupy it believe we have to move too, in our own space."

So the two kinds of movement continue after Henderson meets Dahfu. The ruler seems to "float" gracefully, even when he throws the skulls—he soars while Henderson thinks that *he* sinks. During the ritual "gouts of water like hand grenades burst all about and on him," not destroying but creating Henderson. When Dahfu tells him about cosmic force, the imagery reasserts itself—*man must move; he cannot stand still under blows*. Then it does not matter that Dahfu falls into the cage and is killed. Reality continues to flow, drowning some. But there are spots where it stops for a moment—they are as calm as the pink light. As Henderson thinks: *"Light itself was all Einstein needed."* Perhaps he puts it better this way: "The opposite makes the opposite." Chaos implies order; wildness implies peacefulness. And the last time we see Henderson, he is running "over the pure white lining of the gray Arctic silence." He is a pinpoint of moving light, "a little world made cunningly" of changing order.

Bellow's heroes are obsessed by vision. As "visionaries" they tend to *see* existence in oblique or unbalanced ways; the mirrors into which they peer are frequently distorted. Joseph, the dangling man, is unnaturally self-centered: the "others" reflect his preoccupations; they are inversions of his true image. Thus he sees the athlete, the tough boy, as an alien, who doesn't conform to the right code—his own. Always subject to such hallucinations, he can "reverse" the summer, making himself "shiver in the heat." When he looks at the ugly houses, streets, tracks, he wonders if the "people who lived her were actually a *reflection* of the things they lived among" (my italics). Again self and environment reflect each other: How can Joseph get out of himself and see other things? The question is especially compelling after he regards *himself* as a split image: the Joseph of a year ago—a cold, rigid conformist—and the present Joseph. Which one is real? he asks, knowing that he cannot continue to see himself as fragments. Burns, his old friend, cannot recognize him as *he* cannot recognize himself! Joseph partially recognizes that he has faulty vision: "he made mistakes of the sort people make who see things as they wish to see them or, for the sake of their plans, *must* see them." But he cannot correct it.

Continuing to emphasize the mirrors of self, Bellow gives us Minna's party—everyone here is *indistinct*: the "others remained grouped together indistinctly," we are told, and were recalled as "that fellow with the glasses" or "that pasty-looking couple." Abt, in hypnotizing Minna, dims the lights and closes her eyes—indistinctness leads to blindness. Later we listen to Joseph describing his brother, Amos, and his family. Like the tough boy mentioned earlier, Amos is an

inverted image of his younger brother, who regards
him as a "stranger." Etta, Amos' daughter, bears a
"great resemblance" to Joseph: this resemblance "goes
beyond the obvious similarities pointed out by the
family." Can we not say that Etta, "a vain, self-centered, childish" person perfectly mirrors her uncle,
who also stares at himself? In spanking Etta he also
spanks his own narcissistic image. Brooding about his
niece, Joseph discovers that "the face, all faces, had a
significance for me duplicated in no other object. A
similarity of faces must mean a similarity of nature
and presumably of fate." He recalls his grandfather's
photograph, seeing in it a dim reflection of his own—
one that would "reclaim" him "bit by bit." The grandfather and he are one as Etta and he are one. Life is a
series of mirrors: "Alternatives, and particularly desir-
able alternatives, grow only on imaginary trees." It
takes proper vision to choose the right ones.

Now we can understand why Bellow includes the
"double" (the first of many in his novels). When
Joseph sees a stranger fall from some kind of attack, he
sees himself in the man—the fall reminds him of his
own illness, his mother's death, Aunt Dina's scratching. A "pre-vision," he calls it. It results from his
"melodramatic," fragmented view of existence. Everything is double—his two Josephs, Amos and Joseph—
because life is a broken self-image; true vision, epiphany, is rare. Seeking it, Joseph constantly runs into
distortions, grotesque reflections, as in his dream-dou-
ble: he feels a touch on his back and turns: "Then
that swollen face that came rapidly toward mine until
I felt its bristle and the cold pressure of its nose; the
lips kissed me on the temple with a laugh and groan."
Our seer resembles Brydon of "The Jolly Corner," in
love with a grotesque double, or Poe's William Wil-
son. The interior darkness is dangerous—"only a cat's
eye" can see it truly. So we leave Joseph in his old
room, still not seeing wholly. The room is delusive; it
seems to "dwindle" and become a small square. This

is not a visual trick, he informs us. The visual trick—
like the other ones in the novel—is a *revelation* of life's
"ephemeral agreements." No wonder that Joseph rises
"unsteadily" from his rocker—he sees clearly that life
is a cosmic, distorting, treacherous mirror!

The Victim presents the same kinds of mirrors,
implying that "environment serves as an index for the
exploration of characters' attitudes toward themselves
and their world and at the same time as an index for
the definition of an external life." [12] Asa and Allbee
cannot master reality—if such a thing exists—because
they see only themselves. The very first sentence suggests that true vision is rare in New York City, especially on a night when its citizens become "barbaric
fellahin." Asa Leventhal is the "one-eyed king" in this
"country of the blind." He walks in a foreign land,
Staten Island, seeing a "shimmer of fumes" or a
"sunny" white corridor. He sees the "too bright" eyes
of anxious Elena. All these images prepare us for Asa's
"hallucinations"—for his faulty, self-centered, fragmented vision. His own eyes are clouded—"they
seemed to disclose an intelligence not greatly interested in its own powers." He sees mice darting along
the walls. He gazes at other eyes that seem softer and
larger at night, hoping to find something of value.

After Allbee enters, we are again confronted by the
"double"—this stranger holds Asa's secret desires for
punishment and guilt, reflecting them as the stranger
reflects Joseph's death wish. Unbalanced vision is more
intense now. Asa stares at the double's eyes and sees
universal insanity there; later he stares at the water
and sees inhuman lions. Elena mirrors his mother's
madness and his own; Philip, her son, mirrors his
weakness; Max, his brother, mirrors his abdication of
maturity. "Horrible images" intrude: "hideous cardboard cubicles" painted to resemble wood; men sitting
on mission benches. As Joseph stares at himself (a
"Spirit of Alternatives"), so Asa sees himself: "he was
able to see himself as if through a strange pair of

eyes." "Changed in this way into his own observer," he splits himself. He even *becomes* Allbee when he has "a strange close consciousness" of the other; the "look of recognition Allbee [bends] on him [duplicates] the look in his own." Such epiphanies suggest that each man is his own victim; *master and slave fragment the human image*. Existence is captured fully in the following image: "The imperfections of the pane through which Leventhal gazed suggested the thickening of water at a great depth when one looks up toward the surface."

The mirrors persist in *The Adventures of Augie March*, but they are less destructive. The general pattern is clear: Augie constantly meets people who reflect each other—Einhorn resembles Mintouchian who resembles Thea, etc. His world is a kind of "funhouse." Because his range of experience is so great (and, curiously, so limited to authoritarians), he must avoid becoming another reflection.

Here are some of the images of faulty vision, fragmentation, and distortion. There are several "mirrors" in the first chapter: we see the March family preparing to help Mama get new glasses—Grandma Lausch teaches her children how to get correct vision? Augie mentions the photograph of Grandma's husband; the photograph "doubled back between the portico columns of the full-length mirror." This *doubling back* is evident in all the adventures; it underlies his many comparisons to gods and generals. When he notes, for example, that he can't see his father as a "marble-legged Olympian" or his big mother as a "fugitive of immense beauty," he is suggesting that his friends and relatives are distorted, incorrect reflections of the gods: perfect beauty (or vision) exists in Heaven; earthbound people never see themselves properly. The three monkeys—see no evil, speak no evil, hear no evil —are fragmented deities. Augie begins to travel and meets other mirrors. Anna Coblin insists on seeing him as her own Howard, refusing to perceive that he is not a simple double of her son but a different person. Her religion is described this way: she "had things *segmented, flattened down,* and *telescoped* like the stages and floors of the Leaning Tower" (my italics). A poor visionary with her "own ideas of time and place"! No wonder we see her "bothering the morning mirrors with her looks." Simon resembles her in having an "oriental, bestowing temperament"; he becomes the missing father. Contrasted to him, an inverted image, is Georgie, who doesn't stare at the world; on the contrary, he has a "subtle look" set on who knows what—a "seraphic" appearance.

The "true vision of things is a gift, particularly in times of special disfigurement and world-wide Babylonishness." But faulty vision is everywhere. Augie is taken for Mrs. Renling's lover; he thinks of Mr. Renling as a nightbird that "knows all about daylight" but flies toward darkness; Mama March is blind; Augie cannot become a "sun of the world," "Phoebus's boy" —he remains in the dark; Simon (who undergoes a grotesque metamorphosis) runs through lights and almost kills pedestrians; Caligula wears a hood. The net result of these "intimidations" for Augie is simple: existence, he believes, is double, mysterious, fragmented —as Mintouchian claims: "Do you say a double life? It's secret over secret, mystery and then infinity sign stuck on to that. So who knows the ultimate and where is the hour of truth?"

These images reappear in *Seize the Day*. Tommy sees his distorted reflection in the "darkness and deformations of the glass"; he resembles the hotel across the street, which looks like the "image of itself reflected in deep water." He feels, nevertheless, that fragmentation is better than being an "exact duplicate" of his cousin, who brilliantly conforms to the system. But Tommy cannot see clearly; the environment mirrors his failures: Venice, the agent, resembles him; so do Mr. Rubin and Mr. Rappaport. He wonders how to achieve clear vision. Perhaps Dr. Tamkin, a visionary with "hypnotic power in his eyes," can help him. But the charlatan sees everyone as the "faces on a playing card, upside down either way." Although Tamkin writes in his poem: "Look then right before thee. Open thine eyes and see . . . ," Tommy cannot even make out the figures on the stock-exchange board (resembling Mr. Rappaport who shouts, "I can't see"). Epiphany is rare, but it does occur when Tommy sees his image in the coffin. Can he keep this new vision?

I don't want to pursue the many mirrors in *Henderson the Rain King.* Again the crucial problem is how to achieve *insight*—not an easy task when the hero is surrounded by *duplication* (he is like Lily's father in his suicide threat; the orphan at the end parallels Ricey's child); *grotesque reflection* (the lions are stronger than Henderson; one lion is a killer, unlike the other); *faulty vision* (Willatale *sees* despite her cataract; Henderson sits in darkness); or *peculiarity of light*. But Henderson does have visions: when he sees pink light—all that Einstein needed—he is no longer aware of the upside-down universe of things. Then he sees Deity—reality itself—as two-sided and one at the same time. Light, fire—these move but are steady; they distort but are clear: "The opposite makes the opposite." Or as he pictures his epiphany: *"It is very early in life, and I am out in the grass. The sun flames and swells; the heat it emits is its love, too. I have this self-same vividness in my heart. There are dandelions. I try to gather up this green. I put my love-swollen cheek to the yellow of the dandelions. I try to enter into the green."* Every one, he says later, is "given the components to see: the water, the sun, the air, the earth."

This survey of Bellow's imagery reveals several things: the images are "natural," archetypal, and carefully chosen. Most critics of Bellow's fiction refer to his article, "Deep Readers of the World, Beware!" [13] Here he attacks symbol-hunters, asserting that the

deep reader . . . is apt to lose his head. He falls wildly
on any particle of philosophy or religion and blows it
up bigger than the Graf Zeppelin." [14] He is also against
phony images (which become symbolic). What are
true symbols? "A true symbol is substantial, not accidental. You cannot avoid it, you cannot remove it." [15]
Of course, Bellow is right in rebelling against the
artificial, non-substantial symbol, but he seems to flee
partially from complex issues. The few examples he
offers of true symbols don't tell us enough about "sub-
stantiality"; surely if any object—such as a crippled
limb—reappears in a work of art, we cannot call it
accidental—it is there! He takes no account of *patterns* of meaning. Although he believes the crippled
feet of Oedipus are symbolic, he doesn't see that the
feet join the blindness of Oedipus and Tiresias as part
of a thoroughly developed gestalt.

The argument is perhaps a personal one. When
The Adventures of Augie March appeared, several
critics saw "deep" symbols in it. Anthony West, for
example, claimed that Bellow had "chosen to saddle
himself with . . . a lead weight of Melvillean
symbol." [16] The battle between Simon and Augie was
not real: "Augie has a brother, Simon, who is intent
on money and sex as Augie is on culture and love, not
because families are liable to produce that kind of
clash of personality but because America is split between materialism and idealism." [17] Now, Mr. West is
"over-reading," but he does realize that the novel contains symbols. The question is: What do the symbols
mean? I have suggested that certain images seem to
recur so many times that they form a pattern or cluster
of meaning. It is not dangerous to call Augie a symbol
of America—it is necessary! —to see movement as a
symbolic force in the entire novel.

We should not go to the other extreme and say that
instead of handicapping his fiction with symbolic images, Bellow doesn't use *any*. Bellow himself in "Facts
that Put Fancy to Flight," is for concrete realities—for

social facts—but he asks for a "poetry of fact." [18] In other words, the writer should be realistic, knowing how many floors the Hotel Ansonia has, but he should realize Truth is more than such realism: The writer "may be realistic but not about the things that matter, the arrangements that shape our destiny. In this smaller way to stick to the facts limits him to minor schemes of social history, to satire, to muckraking and leveling, or to the penny psychology of private worlds. To this sort of 'objectivity' writers give all they've got. Strong on experience, they are much, much less strong on the truth." [19]

In my essay I have suggested that Bellow uses "natural" images—movement, resemblance, diseased limbs —but he uses them to portray the truths of existence. These images are shaped to symbolize our destiny. When he uses such exotic ones as those Henderson meets, they are still natural in that particular Africa.

The fascinating thing about these seven images is that because they are so real, they recur in all periods —they are archetypal. The pressures felt by Tommy Wilhelm or Asa Leventhal are "crosses" like the one borne by Christ; the disease appears again and again as a symbol (and fact) of our human condition not only in *Oedipus Rex* (remember Bellow's choice of Oedipus' feet as a true symbol) but in *Moby Dick* or *The Magic Mountain*; the beast is in medieval romance or *Gulliver's Travels*; the voyage is in—you name it. If we read Bellow's fiction with care—even the early *Dangling Man*—we see that as modern as his heroes are, they enact mythic trials. The images make Bellow's novels traditional; at the same time they don't destroy freshness or contemporaneity.

I have broken these images asunder. All seven reinforce one another; they coalesce as we read. The beast *moves* wildly; the crippled limbs *mirror* spiritual disfigurement; the weight *entraps* heroes. This is the terrifying "absurdity" of criticism: it elucidates and fragments a felt pattern of meaning.

5

The Styles

What is especially remarkable about Bellow is his ability to mix styles. *Henderson the Rain King* is, of course, completely unlike *Dangling Man* in terms of style, although both employ similar themes, characters, and images. Here I try to capture Bellow's various styles.

Bellow's fiction—especially *Dangling Man, The Victim,* and *Seize the Day*—contains many "realistic" descriptions of the city:

> In the upper light were small fair heads of cloud turning. The streets in contrast looked burnt out; the chimneys pointed heavenward in openmouthed exhaustion. The turf, intersected by sidewalk, was bedraggled, with the whole winter's deposit of deadwood, match cards, cigarettes, dogmire, rubble. The grass behind the palings and wrought-iron frills was still yellow, although in many places the sun had already succeeded in shaking it into livelier green. And the houses, their doors and windows open, drawing in the freshness, were like old drunkards or comsumptives taking a cure. Indeed, the atmosphere of the houses, the brick and plaster and wood, the asphalt, the pipes and gratings and hydrants outside, and the interiors—curtains and bedding, furniture, striped wallpaper and horny ceilings, the ravaged throats of entry halls and the smeary blind eyes of windows—this atmosphere, I say, was one of an impossible rejuvenation.

Here is the cruel city: the many objects—both inside and outside the houses—are enumerated because Joseph wants to capture the massive burden of things which stunt him (and every individual). These objects are not particularly beautiful—they are, on the contrary, junk. Underlying his description of ugliness is a question: How can society allow people to live in filth and poverty? It is no wonder that the houses are compared to drunkards or comsumptives! Society itself is diseased; it is equally infected—and infects—things and citizens, rendering them powerless.

The striking thing about this passage is that Bellow realizes that *there is no such thing as "realism."* He cannot simply look at the houses and say: How massive! How ugly! How real! "Realism" is a false word because it implies the eye as a camera; but the mind's eye is involved in the picture. There can be no objectivity. Consequently, the passage is colored by value words, by symbolic or connotative language, presented from the view of a *thoughtful* observer. Every sentence demonstrates this quality: one sentence suggests that the clouds—nature itself?—are "fair heads"; they are "good." Sentence two immediately suggests, in contrast, the "evil" of the city—the streets are dark, exhausted; their only hope is that they point toward heaven. Notice that the two sentences are in tense opposition; they enhance the many thematic and imagistic oppositions I have already discussed. The sentences present a humanization of city and clouds: the chimneys have "mouths"; the clouds have (or are) "heads." Further on, we note that the houses are "sick people" and the sun is lively. The environment in Bellow's fiction is always related to the human element—there is never any pure, nonhuman, "naturalistic" description: spiritual involvement is all-important.

Usually Bellow's realistic descriptions depend for their effects on rhythm. Here we have a slow rhythm —all the objects move sluggishly before the mind's eye. There are many qualifications such as: "in contrast," "although in many places," and "I say." Joseph pauses as if he wishes to understand and speak about full implications of the scene. He isn't able to think "on the run"; he must continually clarify. (He states characteristically that the atmosphere is hopeless, even though such a statement is implied in the description itself.) He must *confirm* the thought for himself and his listeners.

Are there any defects in the passage? We can possibly quarrel with the somewhat false assertions: chimneys are *not exhausted*; they don't *point to heaven*. The pathetic fallacy enters. Bellow would probably argue, however, that there is no such fallacy—this is Joseph, a dangling man, looking at himself as he gazes at the city. Naturally, he will see only his own image in the environment because he cannot get out of himself. Another possible defect is the *sameness* of rhythem and tone. Passages like this one occur throughout the novel; they pile up like the "whole winter's deposit." The problem is one of "imitative form"—to use Yvor Winters' phrase. Must Bellow become "dull" to present Joseph's dull existence? Obviously not. But this passage symbolizes the problem he has in *Dangling Man*. I think that he solves it—just barely.

Bellow develops his realistic style. It becomes much more suggestive, "unreal," complex. Although he gives us many other descriptions of the ugly city, he makes them much more fascinating. *The Victim* contains many:

> Leventhal went into the kitchen where Philip sat beside the table on a high stepstool. He had a bowl of dry cereal before him and he poured milk over it, digging up the flap of the milk carton with his thumbnail; he peered and sliced a banana, sprinkled sugar over it, and flipped the skin into the sink with its pans and dishes. The paper frills along the shelves of the cupboard crackled in the current of the fan. It ran on the cabinet, sooty, with insectlike swiftness and a thrum-

ming of its soft rubber blades; it suggested a fly hovering below the tarnish and heat of the ceiling and beside the scaling, many-jointed, curved pipes on which Elena hung rags to dry.

We have seen ugliness in the earlier passage, but the ugliness here is much more interesting. Consider the fan as fly. The image in itself is better than the houses as consumptives: it gives an "unreal" quality to the home atmosphere, suggesting also that Leventhal is more original or "high-strung" than Joseph. The passage is not dull because it is full of unexpected turns; the slow gestures (and rhythm) are varied from the milk being poured to the "insectlike swiftness" of the fan. These subtle changes in movement create a feeling that Bellow no longer cares about set pieces of description. *Reality becomes process*, not stasis as in *Dangling Man*, and it is even more mysterious. We don't know how it will "turn out."

I have noted that even in his realistic passages Bellow becomes impatient with "scientific" description. Ralph Freedman has discussed the change from *Dangling Man* to *The Adventures of Augie March* and *Henderson the Rain King*: "Although the reader still encountered familiar themes dealing with urban middle class life and urban squalor, he found them in unexpected contexts and configurations. Society was no longer only opposed to the hero, whether knowing or blind. Rather, it ironically reflected the hero's consciousness—functioning as his symbolic mirror—while at the same time it also maintained its time-honored place as the source and creator of his condition." [1] Mr. Freedman is correct in his discussion of the great change—a change so great that we marvel at how the same writer could give us *Henderson* and *Dangling Man*. But even in the early novels, as Mr. Freedman later suggests, "fantasy" combats reality, producing great tension in the reader's mind.

The consciousness that subtly inserts itself in physical description in the passages I have quoted bursts forth in dreams. From the dreams of Joseph and Asa to the visions of Henderson—fantasy begins early and continues to the present. It demonstrates that the theme of madness is woven into the texture. As *moha* fits realistic style so does madness fit fantasy!

A few dreams are found in *Dangling Man* after Joseph reaches the "edge of being." These represent his deep longings for punishment or escape from his plight. They occur because he can no longer suppress them. In one he finds himself in a "low chamber with rows of large cribs or wicker bassinets in which the dead of a massacre were lying." He tells his dark guide that he must reclaim one of the bodies but, as an outsider, he doesn't know which one to choose. The other merely smiles at him and says: "It's well to put oneself in the clear in something like this." Then Joseph understands that he is searching for a special one. He continues to walk up the aisle:

> it was more like the path of a gray draught than anything so substantial as a floor. The bodies, as I have said, were lying in cribs, and looked remarkably infantile, their faces pinched and wounded. I do not remember much more. I can picture only the low-pitched, long room much like some of the rooms in the Industrial Museum in Jackson Park; the childlike bodies with pierced heads and limbs; my guide, brisk as a rat among his charges; an atmosphere of terror such as my father many years ago could conjure for me, describing Gehenna and the damned until I shrieked and begged him to stop; and the syllables *Tanza*.

What does the dream mean? Joseph associates his present prison with the tomb—he is really looking for himself in one of the "large cribs." He is dead. But in a strange way he associates this death with childhood —the "childlike bodies"—as if he feels that his life ended before it began. There are two father figures: both are terrifying because they *know* about him; they don't offer sympathy. Another aspect of the dream is Joseph's recognition of *damnation*: not only does he think that he is damned but he believes that his father has sentenced him here—indeed, the Vergil-like guide, the other father, reasserts the sentence, telling him to keep searching for his damned self in the crib. The dream, then, is fantastic, employing classic principles such as condensation and displacement, but it is describing underlying reality—Joseph's unconscious reasons for stasis.

Throughout *The Victim* Asa fantasizes: the "egg race" of life, the lion-slit of the water, his transformation into Allbee. Fantasy plays a bigger part here than in *Dangling Man*; it heralds the "complete" fantasy of *Henderson*. Here is one of Asa's dreams: He is on a boardwalk: the sea is on his right; on his left is an amusement park. He enters a hotel or store to buy rouge for Mary—inside is a "great, empty glitter of glass and metal." A girl demonstrates various shades, "wiping off each in turn with a soiled hand towel." This dream is superficially "pleasant," but it is completely terrifying underneath. Asa wants desperately to buy a gift for his wife; he wants to please her because he needs her. Who is the salesgirl? Is she a double of Mary, or the whore Allbee has slept with in Asa's bed? Does Asa desire the girl? Why do the sea and the amusement park appear? All these questions are not easily answered, but they suggest that Asa's dream contains those elements—safety, normalcy, "transfer" —which he cannot really handle.

Now when we read *Henderson the Rain King*, we see that Bellow "lets go." The fantasy which occurred at crucial points in the early novels is completely in the foreground. The various rituals, gestures, and situations are, in effect, "waking dreams." "Africa" is the dark continent of the mind—anything can happen here: a dwarf can sit on a goddess; a man can "become" a lion; a ruler can speak in Reichian terms. Reality and fantasy are turned upside-down: fantasy is true reality; reality (of, say, Connecticut) is unreal. Thus it is dangerous to ask all the time about *Henderson*: what does it mean? Fantasy implies intimations of meaning which cannot be "logically" grasped—as dreams are never really understood. Bellow is again fusing categories—because there is no such thing as reality in this novel, we are plunged into the position of the hero who *wants* to know the truth. As D. J. Hughes writes about *Lolita* and *Henderson the Rain King*: "in the novels under discussion, the reality which may exist beyond the wish-engendered fantasies of Humbert and Henderson is not at all clear. Their presumed insanity or abnormality does not lead us to a countering rational world; like their heroes, we must discover a reality through their wishes, and we must participate in their serious dreams. Only the excessively confident reader could do otherwise, and these novels are not written for confident readers. As a result, below the comic surface of each book, a desperate tone emerges, and a serious purgation takes place." [2]

Bellow's fiction contains many different kinds of comedy: parody, farce, irony, and "sick" humor. *Dangling Man* is a "bureaucratic comedy"—to quote Joseph. He laughs at his new position in a dark, "solemn" way, knowing how "funny" things are: Here he is, a grown man, living in his room, afraid to do anything! And, furthermore, his wife supports him! It is no wonder that he claims "there is an element of the comic or fantastic in everyone. You can never bring that altogether under control." Perhaps the most grimly comic incidents occur when he speaks to the "Spirit of Alternatives":

"Then only one question remains."
"What?"
"Whether you have a separate destiny. Oh, you're a shrewd wiggler, "said *Tu As Raison Aussi*.
"But I've been waiting for you to cross my corner. Well, what do you say?"

I think I must have grown pale.

"I'm not ready to answer. I have nothing to say to that now."

"How seriously you take this," cried *Tu As Raison Aussi*. "It's only a discussion. The boy's teeth are chattering. Do you have a chill?" He ran to get a blanket from the bed.

Joseph is "comic" because he lacks self-understanding —he, in effect, sees himself slipping on a banana peel. He knows he should laugh but he is afraid. Finally he shrugs ironically, afraid to face his cosmic awkwardness. But his very solemnity—which tends to be "exaggerated"—mocks itself.

The Victim contains the same kind of "comedy." Because Asa and Allbee are "fools," we have a comedy of errors; existence is viewed as a series of mistakes. Consider, for example, this dialogue:

"After the way you've acted I should throw you out. And if you really believe half the things you said to me, you shouldn't want to stay under the same roof. You're a lousy counterfeit."

"Why you have the whole place to yourself. You can put me up," Allbee said smiling. "I wouldn't be inconveniencing you. But if you want me to do this in the right spirit . . . " And to Leventhal's astonishment— he was too confounded when it happened to utter a sound—Allbee sank out of his chair and went to his knees.

Then he shouted, "Get up!"

Allbee pulled himself to his feet.

The comedy arises out of pain; the two are so close that we are afraid to laugh, thinking that we may be called sadistic. But this dialogue *is* comic: two weaklings—both dependent upon each other—quarrel because they don't want to see themselves clearly. Allbee shrewdly exaggerates his dependence by begging; Asa likes to see his demon in this position, but he is made uncomfortable. The dialogue captures the spirit of *The Eternal Husband*: it is serious and almost farcical. Shall we label the comedy as Jewish or Russian?

Here are some Yiddish proverbs: "Your health comes first—you can always hang yourself later." [3] "If God were living on earth, people would break His windows." [4] "Sleep faster, we need the pillows." [5] Here is the opening of Dostoyevsky's *Notes from Underground*: "I am a sick man. . . . I am a spiteful man. I am an unattractive man. I believe my liver is diseased." [6] It does not matter how we label this kind of humor—the important thing is to see that it functions throughout Bellow's early fiction.

The *Adventures of Augie March* is too *lighthearted* to contain such humor. It gives us "caricature"—Bellow uses the word itself to describe Coblin: "he was really a good size himself, sturdy, and bald in a clean sweep of all his hair, his features also big, rounded and flattened, puffy at the eyes which were given to blinking just about to the point of caricature." The minor characters are "sports"—we laugh at them as we do at cartoons. The major characters are also sports, but we get to know them so well that we cannot simply laugh at their appearances, gestures, or voices. We often feel sorry for them as we do for a Walter Mitty. They are fools—stupid, grotesque, but a bit sad. Caricature, sad humor—there are even more kinds of comedy in the novel: farce (as in some of the Mexican scenes), wit (especially when Mintouchian holds forth), and parody.

Perhaps the most impressive statement of Augie's outlook occurs on the last page. After gazing at all the absurdities of existence—including his own position—he understands the ultimate purpose of humor as Asa and Allbee cannot: "That's the *animal ridens* in me, the laughing creature, forever rising up. What's so laughable, that a Jacqueline, for instance, as hard as that by rough forces, will still refuse to lead a disappointed life? Or is the laugh at nature—including eternity—that it thinks it can win over us and the power of hope?" The laughing creature! How simple to say and hard to accept! Augie's ability to laugh saves him. He rises above possible self-indulgence and sees that he is silly—a victim—but this very perception ennobles him. *Comedy, then, is an enigma because it transcends categories of pain or joy; it resolves ambivalence in a mysterious way.*

In *Seize the Day* Tommy Wilhelm is a fool who cannot function in the outside world. He joins Allbee and Joseph—save for the fact that he is more human than they. Although we laugh at him for being so childish—especially when he tries to understand Dr. Tamkin's poem—we feel sorry for him—almost as sorry as he feels for himself. When he calls himself a "fair-haired hippopotamus," we *smile* at him and feel *ashamed.* Thus sad humor.

But this short novel is rich in other kinds of comedy. Bellow *satirizes* Dr. Tamkin as a "typical" psychologist (as Simon March is a typical businessman). He distrusts charlatans who glibly assert that the world is a hospital. Tamkin is caricatured as well—his "shoulders rose in two pagoda-like points." We don't care about his humanity. We *laugh* more easily *at* him.

"The Wrecker" emphasizes another kind of comedy—farce. Here the various actions are so outlandish, exaggerated, and broad that we see the pure *play* involved. How childish! How joyful! Even the stage directions are playful: the city employee *"has a portfolio under his arm—cardboard—and his double-breasted suit is chalk-striped. An eater of clams and drinker of beer. Seeing ladies, he takes the toothpick from his mouth and with same hand removes his hat."* The wrecker enters with hammer *and* hatchet. His dialogue is exaggerated, as when he claims that knocking down the walls is getting rid of "harmful past life." He "frolics" as does Khrushchev who, according to Bellow, "frolics before the cameras, eats, drinks, fulminates and lets himself be taken home." [7]

Henderson the Rain King contains so many kinds of comedy that I can only generalize here. The *farce* of "The Wrecker" is immediately apparent: "Lily is, for instance, entertaining ladies and I come in with my filthy plaster cast, in sweat socks; I am wearing a red velvet dressing gown which I bought at Sulka's in Paris in a mood of celebration when Frances said she wanted a divorce. In addition I have on a red wool hunting cap." But there is also *satire* as when Henderson describes his "typical" American marriage (a divorce of interests): Lily and the kids leave the dirty house and go for a ride in the country; Henderson stays at home. The entire novel is a *parody* of ancient quests. D. J. Hughes has indicated: "Henderson himself calls up, either directly or in a parodic mode, Oedipus, Moses, Joseph, Jacob, Falstaff, Lear, etc., and his entire quest has a familiar mythic pattern. But the novel never sinks under its airy symbolic weight; as in *Lolita* the prevailing comic texture provides an atmosphere in which the serious symbol appears transparent." [8] And there is the *wit*, the verbal play, of those "impossible" dialogues of Dahfu and Henderson:

> I said to the king, "And how does Obersteiner's allochiria and all that medical stuff you gave me to read come into this?"
> He patiently said, "All the pieces fit properly. It will presently be clear. But first by means of the lion try to distinguish the states that are given and the states that are made. Observe that Atti is all lion. Does not take issue with the inherent. Is one hundred percent within the given."

Such philosophical conversation is delightful. We like hearing them communicate, wondering what they will say next.

Throughout this book I have hinted how close Bellow is to other contemporary writers and thinkers—to Mann, Reich, Freud, etc. His insistence upon the joy of play—for this is where his comedy is headed—links him to J. Huizinga who, in *Homo Ludens*, has suggested that play is all around us—whether we realize it or not. Huizinga seems to imply, in fact, that if only we could realize the "seriousness" of play, we would be much improved. His words help us to appreciate the intention of Bellow in *Henderson the Rain King.*

> Since the reality of play extends beyond the sphere of human life it cannot have its foundations in any rational nexus, because this would limit it to mankind. The incidence of play is not associated wth any particular stage of civilization or view of the universe. Any thinking person can see at a glance that play is a thing on its own, even if his language possesses no general concept to express it. Play cannot be denied. You can deny, if you like, nearly all abstractions; justice, beauty, truth, goodness, mind, God. You can deny seriousness, but not play.
>
> But in acknowledging play you acknowledge mind, for whatever else play is, it is not matter. Even in the animal world it bursts the bounds of the physically existent. From the point of view of a world wholly determined by the operation of blind forces, play would be altogether superfluous. Play only becomes possible, thinkable and understandable when an influx of *mind* breaks down the absolute determinism of the cosmos. The very existence of play continually confirms the supralogical nature of the human situation. Animals play, so they must be more than merely mechanical things. We play and know that we play, so we must be more than merely rational beings, for play is irrational.[9]

In Bellow's fiction there are many pastoral passages which imply that even city dwellers can achieve a rare moment of peace in the natural scene. But these don't assert that nature-worship can solve the various dualities of existence (man and nature are opposites)—nature is occasionally a healer; *the cure is never complete.*

Although nature is rather dismal at the beginning of *Dangling Man*—"the streets at this time of the year are forbidding, and then, too, I have no overshoes"—it is less so at the end. Winter turns to spring. The new season "resurrects" Joseph: "The air had a brackish smell of wet twigs and moldering brown seed pods, but it was soft, and through it rose, with indistinct but thrilling reality, meadows and masses of trees, blue and rufous stone and reflecting puddles." Indistinct but thrilling reality! This is what nature holds for the city dwellers! Because the seasons change, they signify that human beings can also change. Joseph is moved —in honor of spring—to "clean up for supper." Perhaps the most thrilling aspect of nature is light. Throughout the "bad" season, he is gloomy, dark— like the atmosphere. Spring brings new light, new vision. As he tells us: "Vision enlarged, red was rough and bloody, yellow clear but thin, blue increasingly warm." The "sun's own yellow" electrifies him. Unfortunately, his dark spirits return as he revisits his old room.

The Victim has the same kind of plot movement. It begins in the "sweltering" New York summer—with the air heavy and "tropical." Leventhal goes to the park to find relief, but there he only finds that dark "nature-spirit," Allbee. Rarely does Asa see light or feel cool winds: "Better to be in the dark." When he does feel better, he sees a "brilliant" morning with its "simple contrasts, white and blue, shining and darkened." Later the afternoon sun looks pale; there is a "current of brackish air" on the ferry. He dreams of "broad, open summer weather," but his dream is interrupted by the choking fumes of gas. Such contraries of nature are never resolved: *there is not one bracing light—only hints of such brilliance.* Marcus Klein puts the matter this way:

> Asa Leventhal, locked in New York's inhuman heat, has moments of freshness and deep breathing at sea on the Staten Island ferry and the plot of the novel moves him toward the relief that will come with Labor Day. The attempted suicide of his antagonist, Allbee, on the eve of that day makes possible Leventhal's birth

into a possible world, and the day itself brings cooling breezes. Nature as transcendent reality brushes Leventhal lightly once—for a brief moment of half-sleep he feels the whole world present to him and about to offer him a mysterious, it would seem redeeming, discovery. But the discovery blows by him and at the end of his action, having abandoned ultimate questioning and now re-entering a darkened theatre with his wife, he is no closer to a notion of reality.[10]

Although *The Adventures of Augie March* is also cyclical, it moves toward light and open nature and leaves us there (before the cycle begins again). First we find Augie in the crowded city—a "somber" place —aware that he is different from a Crusoe, "alone with nature, under heaven." There are hints of pastoral— Augie sees the town gloom end "in a flaming blue teeter of fresh water"—but the first complete communion with bracing nature occurs after he goes to the country resort with Mrs. Renling. Here he "soaks in the heavy nourishing air and this befriending atmosphere like rich life-cake, the kind that encourages love and brings on a mild pain of emotions." He is resurrected; the sunshine removes his city-illusions. Then he plunges into the city gloom again—we have the "barbarous," "raw" winter, images of a "dark Westminster of a time." Mexico has "flamy brilliance," and "momentarily" awakens Augie. But the brilliance is almost too great for him—he is, after all, a city-boy, not used to such hot beauty. The end of the novel captures wonderfully the doubleness of Nature: it offers darkness and light, heaviness and motion. It suggests hopefully that pastoral comfort lies ahead, if Augie can "beat the dark."

The city-country opposition appears in *Seize the Day*. Cramped by pressures of New York, Tommy Wilhelm dreams of nature as a healing force. When he worked with the Rojax Corporation, he had a small apartment in Roxbury. There was a porch; "on mornings of leisure, in late spring weather like this, he used to sit expanded in a wicker chair with the sunlight pouring through the weave, and sunlight through the slug-eaten holes of the young hollyhocks and as deeply as the grass allowed into small flowers. This peace (he forgot that the time had had its troubles, too), this peace was gone." (Note the recurrence of light!) The country is a dim hope for Tommy, but he cannot stop thinking of it. "The easy tranquil things of life" can be recovered; Mt. Serenity waits. As Tamkin says: "Creative is nature. Rapid. Inspirational." But the real irony is that "pastoral" is achieved in a dark funeral chapel.

There are things, Henderson thinks, that a "man never forgets and afterward truly values"—such things as the Mediterranean, the "towering softness of the water." Pastoral is sought constantly. Half of the time Henderson is confused by the deceptions, motions, and violence of nature—as in the rainfall scene—but he manages to find softness, even as his teeth itch: "they say the air is the final home of the soul but I think that as far as the senses go you probably can't find a sweeter medium than water." Water, air, light —these elements are necessary for pastoral. Usually there is a combination of the three as when Henderson mentions the peaceful "mild pink color, like the water of watermelon" which makes him reach a still point. (The pink is opposed to the *twilight* vision of the octopus.) Slowly the three elements come to the foreground until finally Henderson sees the "white of the Arctic" in Atti, the lion, the light Einstein needed, and the "white lining of the gray Arctic silence." Unlike *The Victim* which ends in a darkening theatre, *Henderson the Rain King* (and *The Adventures of Augie March*) ends with fast-moving but peaceful pastoral. Quite a change!

Although I have discussed the real and fantastic descriptions, the comic thrusts, and the dramatic images of Bellow's novels, I have not stressed enough the style

which *orders* description. In *Aspects of the Novel*
E. M. Forster discusses prophecy:

> With prophecy in the narrow sense of foretelling
> the future we have no concern, and we have not much
> concern with it as an appeal for righteousness. What
> will interest us today—what we must respond to, for
> interest now becomes an appropriate word—is an accent
> in the novelist's voice, an accent for which the flutes
> and saxophones of fantasy may have prepared us. His
> theme is the universe, or something universal, but he is
> not necessarily going to "say" anything about the uni-
> verse; he proposes to sing, and the strangeness of song
> arising in the halls of fiction is bound to give us a
> shock.[11]

Prophecy, Mr. Forster continues, is a "tone of voice. It
may imply any of the faiths that have haunted humanity—Christianity, Buddhism, dualism, Satanism, or
the mere raising of human love and hatred to such a
power that their normal receptacles no longer contain
them." [12] Prophecy is not easy to attain. It demands
"humanity and the suspension of the sense of
humor." [13] Even if these two qualities are attained,
there is another requirement. Mr. Forster distin-
guishes between the "prophet" and the "preacher."
For the preacher he chooses George Eliot; for the
prophet, Dostoevsky: "George Eliot talks about God,
but never alters her focus; God and the tables and
chairs are all in the same plane, and in consequence
we have not for a moment the feeling that the whole
universe needs pity and love. . . . In Dostoevsky the
characters and situations always stand for more than
themselves; infinity attends them; though yet they remain individuals they expand to embrace it and sum-
mon it to embrace them." [14]

When we look at Bellow's "prophetic" style, we
find that he has developed it (as he has done the other
styles). *Dangling Man* contains many passages written
by a preacher, not a prophet. Here is Joseph viewing
Minna's party:

The party blared on inside, and I began to think what a gathering of this sort meant. And it came to me all at once that the human purpose of these occasions had always been to free the charge of feeling in the pent heart; and that, as animals, instinctively sought salt or lime, we, too, flew together at this need as we had at Eleusis, with rites and dances, and at other high festivals and corroborees to witness pains and tortures, to give our scorn, hatred, and desire temporary liberty and play.

Joseph is telling us what his experience *means;* he is too intellectual to make us respond to "eternity." He is not transported, although he would like to be. His slowness—his very *rhythm* itself—inhibits his prophetic tone. The passage is, consequently, a bit artificial. But there are passages of true prophecy in the novel. One such passage occurs when Joseph gazes—no, stares!—at the fallen man, wondering: "Would the red face go gray, the dabbled hands stop their rowing, the jaw drop?" The questions move him. He suddenly sees his own "fallen" past: images of flight, destruction, and silence blur his mind. Then he thinks: "We live, great weight on our faces, straining toward the last breath which comes like the gritting of gravel under a heavy tread." The entire passage is beautifully written: Bellow lifts us from the shocking present to the equally shocking past; we respond to images before we get the message—indeed, the images *embody* the message.

The opposition of preaching and prophecy—another opposition to add to our list!—occurs in the novels after *Dangling Man.* Prophecy wins in *The Victim.* Here there are fewer artificial comments; the ideas arise dramatically: demons speak suddenly. Bellow handles the dialogues about universal disorder with greater care: Allbee, for example, bursts forth with such prophecies as "Hot stars and cold hearts, that's your universe." Perhaps the very fact that Schlossberg as moral guide must get his comments across makes him a "false" prophet—when he enters, we are ready for preaching. Despite these minor flaws in prophetic *dialogue, The Victim* shakes us because of the unexpected, fantastic turns of phrase or idea.

We are so moved by Asa's unbalanced nature that when he has visions, we *know* them as we do not with Joseph:

> We were all the time taking care of ourselves, laying up, storing up, watching out on this side and on that side, and at the same time running, running desperately, running as if in an egg race with the egg in a spoon. And sometimes we were fed up with the egg, sick of it, and at such a time would rather sign on with the devil and what they called the powers of darkness than run with the spoon, watching the egg, fearing for the egg.

The powers of darkness capture Asa. He is so involved that he cannot slow down; he must keep pace with his vision. Thus he runs through his sentences (as does man with his egg): present participles abound; few qualifications exist. Perhaps Asa is less of a thinker than Joseph, responding more fearfully and quickly (as does the other when he sees the man fall). When he prophesies, we feel that his whole life—his very being—is at stake. He hasn't the energy to be logical.

The Adventures of Augie March is prophetic. At every point in the novel the hero vibrates to the "music of the spheres." When he gazes at, say, the white and gray of Belgium, seeing himself as an *animal ridens* and Columbus, he captures the universal longings we all have; he is a "natural" visionary. But at other times, especially in the dialogues about truth, freedom, etc., Augie is preaching to us. (Perhaps he is trying to convince himself.) When he explains his philosophy of the "axial lines of life," he is so involved with his language, his associations of thought, that he belabors a simple idea just to hear himself talk. Then he gives us explanation, not ecstasy. The novel is split between the two. What is memorable is the sudden, joyful insight into universal freedom; what is not is the dull philosophy. Like Whitman, Augie is better "on the road"; there he is not interested in *explaining* what he has seen.

One of the reasons for the split is this: Augie is so enamored of his language—so "narcissistic"—that he cannot get out of himself. He lacks humility—E. M. Forster's requirement—at times. It is, of course, dangerous to link Bellow with Augie, but the very fact that Joseph *and* Augie like to hear themselves talk means that involvement with self—can we call it preaching?—reappears because Bellow has not given up a vice. Often when Augie expounds his message, we are tempted to admonish him (and Bellow): *Get going. See; don't think about seeing.*

Fortunately, Tommy Wilhelm does not have Augie's self-confidence. He cannot pursue a philosophical question at great length. Tommy Wilhelm *feels* things deeply—like Asa he is less intellectual than Joseph and Augie. He is a haunted man, always responding to the destructive world with dreams, fantasies, and visions. He prays suddenly: "Let me out of this clutch and into a different life. For I am all balled up. Have mercy." The desperate quality of his prayer demonstrates that he has no time for preaching.

Bellow juxtaposes the weak prophet to Dr. Tamkin. The latter talks and talks; he even writes poems about his visions. Because of the tensions between the two men, we recognize basic separation of words and deeds. The split in *The Adventures of Augie March* is avoided—in fact, taken advantage of—by having two characters as "visionaries." When Dr. Tamkin speaks, we understand that he cannot *see*, although he would like to: "The interest of the pretender soul is the same as the interest of the social life, the society mechanism. This is the main tragedy of human life." Tommy recognizes himself *enacting* Tamkin's ideas; he *embodies* principles. Thus we are ready for complete prophecy when Tommy is away from the false preacher and *stares at himself*. Not looking for universal truth, he finds it in his own heart: "The flowers and lights fused ecstatically in Wilhelm's blind, wet eyes; the heavy sea-like music came up to his ears. It poured into him where he had hidden himself in the center of a crowd by the great and happy oblivion of tears. He heard it and sank deeper than sorrow, through torn sobs and cries toward the consummation of his heart's ultimate need."

Although we may enjoy the witty conversations of Dahfu and Henderson, at first, after a while they tend to be repetitive and "prosaic." They are, finally, less impressive than the prophetic visions of Henderson during the rain festival, in the lion tunnel, and at the airport—action which is more lively and divine than the preaching of Dahfu. *Henderson the Rain King* demonstrates the ambivalence arising from preaching versus prophecy; it is somewhat broken.

This survey of styles helps us to appreciate Bellow's great imagination. He refuses to rest in one style; he affirms that there is more than one way—realistic, fantastic, or comic—of responding to life. His fiction echoes his insistence (in essays and reviews) upon imaginative, dynamic freedom.

Often Bellow uses his non-fiction to praise the "shaping spirit." Hemingway's style, he tells us, reflects the "fearful struggle of a deaf, isolated, self . . . to work out a style of survival." [15] This style is, in effect, the "effective form" no longer provided by "churches or orders of chivalry or systems of education." [16] It is an independent, meaningful gesture. Dreiser "depended on principle, not taste." [17] Bellow can accept the "tasteless" quality of his novels because it signifies a personal struggle to overcome reality, shaping it—although awkwardly or brutally—to his own ends. Dreiser is an example of an individual driving "beyond the ordinary limitations of his type." [18] He is a culture-hero. These comments on other writers are perhaps less revealing than Bellow's comments on his own writing. In "Distractions of a Fiction Writer" he writes that he—as does any novelist—"begins with disorder and disharmony, and he goes toward order by an unknown process of the imagination." [19] Mere experience—life itself—is not enough. The writer, he tells us elsewhere, "must not expect life to bind itself to be stable for his sake or to accommodate his ambitions." [20] Imagination is that human force which orders raw experience into artistic truth: "Therefore the important humanity of the novel must be the writer's own. His force, his virtuosity, his powers of poetry, his reading of fate are at the center of his book. The reader is invited to bring his sympathies to the writer rather than the characters, and this makes him something of a novelist too." [21]

Returning to Bellow's styles, we see that they incarnate his reading of fate. I have suggested that he is concerned with the tensions, oppositions, and polarities of existence—*moha* versus spirit; time versus eternity; Jew versus Gentile; fathers versus sons; men versus women; rooms versus voyages; and reflections versus themselves. It is appropriate that his various styles—although clearly one or two dominate any novel—oppose one another. They are "human," clamoring for attention, wanting to take the center of the stage. Because they are always present, they make the confident reader uncomfortable. They dramatize for him the "painful" struggles of existence. They show him that humor is not far from naturalism—life is a cycle. That these styles are *organized* and *mastered* symbolizes an even deeper message: the novelist, like his readers, can govern his problems and internal wars. *In that shaping process lies sanity, freedom, power— what Bellow's own characters seek—and victory itself.* Can any writer do more than "substantiate" this deep truth?

6

Herzog

In *Herzog* Bellow employs his usual themes, characters, and images, but he is able to transform—or, better yet, expand—them so that they assume new life.

Perhaps the best introduction to the themes of the novel is this long quotation. Herzog is trying to explain what forces move him:

> But how was he to describe this lesson? The description might begin with his wild internal disorder, or even with the fact that he was quivering. And why? Because he let the entire world press upon him. For instance? Well, for instance, what it means to be a man. In a city. In a century. In transition. In a mass. Transformed by science. Under organized power. Subject to tremendous controls. In a condition caused by organization. In a condition caused by mechanization.

He is "quivering" because he cannot tolerate the pressures of organization. Things "press" upon him; they limit his control. Although he may believe at first with Joseph or Asa Leventhal that it is urban life which unsettles him, he realizes that he cannot stop with such simple causes. The grinding noises of machinery; the "desperately purposeful crowds"; the crazy money-flow—these things are symbols of *moha* itself which condemns him to anxiety. But Herzog cannot take the open road; he has responsibilities to his chil-

dren (and to himself). He cannot be as "larky" as
Augie March. He must stay where he is and endure
these organized external pressures.

Herzog is "mad"—his mental state is emphasized in
the very first line of the novel—because he distrusts
"the others": "reality instructors" plot against him;
they use him to further their own ends. It is mislead-
ing, however, to accuse him of paranoid feelings because he does see things accurately. He knows that he
is a plaything to the various lawyers, psychiatrists, and
masqueraders. He wishes at times to withdraw from
these battles. But his withdrawal into cozy narcissism
—consider, for example, his bathroom rituals and his
new-found interest in clothing—cannot flourish. He
can never really escape. He moves erratically from
open hostility to warm privacy; this very movement is
"unbalanced" because he views himself as passive object. And he delights in retelling the story of his
"wretched" existence so much—especially his betrayal
by Madeline and Valentine—that it begins to assume
a life of its own. It becomes his "ideal construction."
Thus he joins Bellow's other madmen who also fall in
love with ideal constructions and tend to live in compulsive, abstract ways. His internal pattern is as destructive as the patterns others impose upon him.

It is only when Herzog remembers his past in the
slums of Montreal that he regains some sanity. He
visualizes at length childhood incidents; he relives
them. He is in touch with the "eternal return" in the
same way Henderson is with the lion cub at the end of
his adventures; and he can, therefore, forget, if only
momentarily, the pressures and lies which presently
surround him. Time—and life itself—*opens* for him.
This is not to imply that he (or Bellow) is mystical—
the "eternal return" is rooted in unconscious revelation. When he sees the childbeaters in the courtroom,
he can think not only of June, his daughter, but of his
own childhood. (More of this later.)

Herzog believes that time, Jewishness, and "family

feeling" are inextricably bound, even though he never consciously admits this fact. When he is tender towards others (regarding them as "relatives"), he uses Yiddish expressions; when he remembers his childhood, he thinks of Jewishness as a *creative, timeless, special feeling.* Unlike Augie or Joseph he can accept —indeed, he longs to accept—his heritage as the solution to his problems. His religious transcendence—if it can be called that—lies in his ability to find "divinity at home." Consider the following passage:

> Napolean Street, rotten, toylike, crazy and filthy, riddled, flogged with harsh weather—the bootlegger's boys reciting ancient prayers. To this Moses' heart was attached with great power. Here was a wider range of human feelings than he had ever again been able to find. The children of the race, by a never-failing miracle, opened their eyes on one strange world after another, age after age, and uttered the same prayer in each, eagerly loving what they found.

Several values are evident here. Childhood holds ancient truths; prayers are less important as orthodox ritual than as heartfelt utterance; the heart (or sane humanity?) is "miraculous." Herzog emphasizes "children of the race," and this emphasis represents a dramatic change from Bellow's earlier, indirect presentations. In *Dangling Man* and *Augie March* "Jewishness" is not detailed at length; in *The Victim* it is assimilated to some universalist principle; in *Henderson the Rain King* it fuses with Reichian mysticism. Only here does it become, even more forcefully than in *Seize the Day, a persistent guiding light.*

Herzog writes to the Lord: *"How my mind has struggled to make coherent sense. I have not been too good at it. But have desired to do your unknowable will, taking it, and you without symbols. Everything of intensest significance. Especially if divested of me."* He cannot believe in orthodox doctrines, but he can find the measure of ultimate truth in "everything of

intensest significance"—especially in his first family
and his Montreal past. The latter *are* symbols of True
Feeling; they are as close to transcendence as he can
get. It is comparatively easy to maintain that such
religion is mere sentimentality and cliché. Both Herzog and Bellow are a bit lazy; they make convenient
connections between the family and the Lord's Will.
They neglect the fact that divinity is above the family.
Do they confuse the two because of some *driving need*
to see salvation at home? Perhaps I am belaboring the
point; it is important enough to see Jewishness—even
if it is vaguely defined as family feeling or heartfelt
truth—play such an impressive role in this most recent
novel.

Superficially Herzog is "divorced" from all the others
who want to teach him about reality—especially his
second wife, Madeline, who lives with their daughter
(and, when he can leave his own wife, Valentine Gersbach). He is another "bachelor."

Herzog cannot get along well with women. Either
he submits to their warm advances, or he rebels
against their strong wills. He is constantly afraid. Although he admires Ramona's company—she knows
how to offer food and sex—he realizes that her insights
into his problems are rather limited. He needs more
than sexual delight and material comfort. He writes
but never mails a letter to her: "*You are a great comfort to me. We are dealing with elements more or less
stable, more or less controllable, more or less mad. It's
true. I have a wild spirit in me though I look meek and
mild. You think that sexual pleasure is all this spirit
wants, and since we are giving him that sexual pleasure, then why shouldn't everything be well?*" He cannot accept pleasure as the cure; he distrusts the easy
reductionism of Ramona and her mentors. In this
respect he repeats similar complaints of other "bache-
lors" in Bellow's fiction who would like to forget their

problems by means of sex, but who cannot relinquish their wild, inquiring spirits.

Nor can Herzog live peacefully with Madeline. She attempts to assert her masculine will. She distrusts sex; she desires power. She is able to use one for the other —as in her relationships with him and Valentine—but she is never satisfied to let things stand. She is "on the move," compulsively discovering new worlds or men to conquer. She changes roles constantly (unlike Ramona who offers the safety of one clearly-defined role). She converts; she becomes a graduate student; she changes her fashions: "*Conversion was a theatrical event for Madeline. Theatre—the art of upstarts, opportunists, would-be aristocrats . . . Obviously she had religious feeling but the glamour and the social climbing were more important.*" Madeline resembles Thea Fenchel in *The Adventures of Augie March* and Margaret in *Seize the Day*. She also exerts power over men who fight it reluctantly. But she is more carefully described—the hostility makes her portrait extremely vivid—and she stands as the archetype of domineering women who "eat green salad and drink human blood."

Because Herzog unconsciously sees himself as a "child" before Ramona and Madeline, he despises Phoebe Gerbach, Valentine's wife, as an image of himself. They cannot converse because each secretly longs for and is repelled by the other. She unconsciously admires his concern with matters of truth and betrayal; such concern, however, could shatter the blissful pattern which she believes. He sees her weakness, and, at times, he wants to yield to it—to forget the entire sordid situation. He says: "Some people are *sentenced* to certain relationships. Maybe every relationship is either a joy or a sentence." Their partners have sentenced them to this tense, ambiguous relationship.

Herzog cannot get along well with men. They are the bearers of power and justice; they fight his grand

insights. Dr. Edvig, the psychiatrist, treats him as a
case. He maintains that he is a "reactive-depressive"
tending to form "frantic dependencies." By delighting
"calmly" in the world's sorrow, he keeps himself intact. The various judges, policemen, and lawyers also
consider Herzog a plaything. His feelings are not important before the Law—only his apparent "wrong-
doing" matters. It is true that they misread his motives (as does Dr. Edvig) because they assume that
human actions are "pure." Herzog carries a gun; he
therefore means to do harm. Herzog is ill; he therefore
cannot care for his child. They settle for "official
truth." These various "reality instructors" are related
to statesmen who rule the world in simplistic ways,
employing individuals as pawns in irrational games
sanctioned as national policy. Herzog as "right-think-
ing citizen" cannot stop them; he cannot even vote
them out of office. These reasons compel him to
think: *In every community there is a class of people
profoundly dangerous to the rest. I don't mean the
criminals. For them we have punitive sanctions. I
mean the leaders. Invariably the most dangerous people seek the power.*

And Herzog cannot cope with his "spiritual fathers." They sacrifice him to their own truths. Valentine Gersbach may exaggerate his beliefs (and, on
occasion, his style), but he does so only to further his
own ends. Imitating him—becoming a "second Herzog"—he wins Madeline. In one passage he is said to
be "a prophet, a *Shofat,* yes, a judge in Israel, a king."
Valentine is a false prophet; his visions are his own
theatrical suggestions. But it is especially interesting
that he is linked, although ironically, to official guardians. The implication is that he joins them in masquerade and manipulation. Will, Herzog's real brother,
does not want to destroy Herzog for any fiendish (or
prophetic?) plans. He also regards him, however, as
less the well-rounded citizen than as the "case." He
cannot tolerate eccentricity because it interferes with

his sense of the right way. He "humors" him. He recognizes the impracticality and foolishness of the Ludeyville house, seeing it as a symbol of dangerous "madness." Of course, he is partially right, but he doesn't see that the house is organically related to Herzog and, therefore, *right for him.* Herzog thinks: *"Myself is thus and so, and will continue thus and so. And why fight it? My balance comes from instability. Not organization or courage, as with other people."* Perhaps this passage summarizes the difference between Herzog and his well-meaning brother: his lack of organization (or instability) threatens the usual visions of business, because it suggests that poetic inspiration is as important as "facts and figures."

What explains Herzog's divorce from the various "spiritual fathers" and "exotic" women? Why can't he accept their "reality-instructions"? Why does their power—indeed, power itself—trouble him? We must read between the lines to see the roots of his divorce in his relationship to his parents. I have suggested previously that the parents of Bellow's heroes are not allowed to appear at great length. In this novel the usual pattern is broken.

We see Herzog's mother several times. She cared more for her son(s) than she did for herself. She spoiled him: "She certainly spoiled me. Once, at nightfall, she was pulling me on the sled, over crusty ice, the tiny glitter of snow, perhaps, four o'clock of a short day in January. Near the grocery we met an old baba in a shawl who said, 'Why are you pulling him, daughter!'" She performed "unnecessarily"; she gave of herself so much that she became tired. Herzog remembers her wasting away. (Notice the linkage in his mind between sacrifice and death.) As she drew near death, she grew "mournful," but she cared more about the effect of him than on herself as she said: "That's right, Moses I am dying now." She changed into earth—as she had once explained that we are born of earth, she rubbed her finger, "rubbed until something dark appeared on the deep-lined skin, a particle of what certainly looked to him like earth." Self-sacrifice, mourning, and "earthiness"—these qualities make a lasting impression on him. When we meet Herzog in his later years, we discover that he cannot relate to women who try to dominate him. They, unlike his mother, use deception to gain power! They try to destroy him! (He can admire Ramona only when he thinks of her "family feeling" as she cares for her aunt.) He must unconsciously associate women with simple homecoming; he is unsure about how to act when they compete with him. He seeks always to recapture the memory of "good old days" with his mother.

The situation is more dramatic with his father. Jonah Herzog emigrated from Russia to Canada; there he tried various jobs but he could not do well in any of them until he became a bootlegger of whiskey over the border. Even this job didn't suit him; he was made for "finer things." Herzog remembers one incident in which his "late unlucky" father was "hijacked, beaten up, and left in a ditch. Father Herzog took the worst beating because he resisted. The hijackers tore his clothes, knocked out one of his teeth, and trampled him." The incident has great significance. His father, "a sacred being, a King" was "destroyed," and in the process, *he* confronted cruelty and injustice in the world. He did not forget these things. He grew up to be ambivalent about power, fearing and desiring it. When he recalls the incident in later years, he believes that at least his father's "claim to exceptional suffering"—to "his rags, his bruises"—was somehow noble or personal; "we are on a more brutal standard now, a new terminal standard, indifferent to persons."

Herzog also remembers another incident. His father threatened him (one year before his death) with a gun. "He had no patience with Moses." He could not tolerate his errors; he became enraged when he was asked for a loan. "Idiot! Calf!" he screamed. "Don't come to my funeral!" Although he did not shoot, he never really forgave him. As Herzog remembers—or, better yet, *relives*—this painful scene, he is on his way to shoot Valentine and Madeline with the same gun. Of course, we know that he cannot kill them (or himself) because he has learned to be terrified by physical violence—both he and his long-suffering father fear powerful laws, official guardians.

Now that we understand his relationship to his parents, we can see why Herzog identifies with the "oppressed." He regards himself as a child before the Law; in the courtroom when he hears of childbeating he feels compassion not only for the child concerned but for his own daughter and himself. He rushes to Chicago to save her and to kill Valentine and Madeline, the "tyrannical lawgivers" (and law-breakers). But as I have mentioned, he cannot kill them because he would, unconsciously, be killing his father who once threatened him with the same gun. He would destroy a loving relationship—and this kind of relationship is rare enough. It is ironic that soon after, he almost kills his daughter and himself in the automobile accident.

When we last encounter Herzog, he has returned to his Ludeyville house. He is in the "parental" hands of the Tuttles. Mr. Tuttle is jokingly referred to as the "master spirit of Ludeyville" who "runs everything." Can't we see in his great ability to do everything skillfully, a sly symbol? Unlike the official fathers Herzog has known, he can take care of him without exerting power in any overbearing way; he is simply there— quietly, efficiently. Bellow, in other words, leaves us with a recuperating Herzog who has recognized his own ambivalent tensions toward authority—the root of his madness—and who is now learning to live with them under the inspirational sway of Mr. Tuttle: "*I will do no more to enact the peculiarities of life. This is done well enough without my special assistance.*"

It is difficult to discuss the imagery of *Herzog*. The various images I have charted previously are here, but they are not so obvious, dense, or plotted as they are in the earlier novels.

Herzog bears the weight of existence: he "had fallen under a spell." He thinks constantly of being crushed. He has to carry the city's noises, crowds, and machines; the knowledge of past defeats; and his daily burdens. He remembers the agony of Valentine "under the wheels of the boxcar"; his "burden of guilt" in not reviewing Shapiro's monograph; and these suggest, in turn, the "layers upon layers of reality" which include "loathsomeness, arrogance, and deceit." These various images of weight (real and symbolic) are related to ones of imprisonment. When we first see Herzog, he is imprisoned in the Ludeyville house, surrounded by scaly walls, mouse droppings, and rat-chewed bread slices. He is in "the coop of privacy" (as he is throughout the novel). Then he remembers Wanda, the Polish woman, and her "happy" entrapment in marriage; and this leads to his view of Warsaw: "The sun was shut up in a cold bottle. The soul shut up inside me. Enormous felt curtains kept the drafts out of the hotel lobby." The sun and human society are locked-up; neither offers a real way out. Herzog sees Ramona as a kindly jailer, Madeline and Valentine as unkindly ones who trapped him without his knowledge, and Nachman imprisoned by the cruelty of the world. The "cries of the soul" lie "in the breast, and in the throat. The mouth wants to open wide and let them out." (They are as buried as the loot Willie Sutton hides in Flushing Meadows.) Later these cries congest his heart in the courtroom scene. Only when he accepts life as imprisonment does he regard the Ludeyville house as his true residence. At the end of the novel, he moves back to this place hoping to give it new life—to make this seeming "dungeon" and "asylum."

Although Bellow gives us images of "stasis," he is more interested in violent, erratic movement. Herzog moves from Chicago to Ludeyville to Europe (in his memories), searching desperately for a "still point." Before he accepts Ludeyville as the place of rest, he is whirled around continually by his emotions and his thoughts. Let us look at these. Early in the novel Herzog yearns "for the Atlantic—the sand, the brine flavor, the therapy of cold water"; he is impressed by the "smooth motion" of the elevator in his New York apartment. Both the Atlantic and the efficient, "greased tracks" of the elevator represent freedom and power. They are opposed to the frenetic movement of money "passing" through him; the "crashing, stamping pile-driving" machines of the city (which reflect his own perceptions?); the "fall into the quotidian" that bothers him; the "explosions of blood" from horrible wars of this century. Can we move *steadily*? Can we evolve (move upward) as de Chardin believes or must we be continually *thrown by violence*? Such questions are suggested. Finally Herzog believes that although the body (and life itself) threatens to "rush away from us," it is somehow balanced. This view steadies his inner turmoil so much that we last see him on a sofa—he is relaxed as he listens to the "steady scratching"—the purposeful movement—of Mrs. Tuttle's broom.

Herzog, the man of "reflection," looks at himself so much that he cannot separate real from the false. He blinds himself (or is blinded). He has to learn to see accurately; the various images help us to grasp his plight and his progress. Although Herzog accuses Madeline and Valentine of "theatre in their looks," he is also theatrical. He calls "upon his eccentricities for relief." He "looks at his garden work with detachment [or so he thinks] as if he were looking through the front end of a telescope at a tiny clear image." Often he pauses before mirrors, watching himself as he changes his clothing and facial expressions. (So do the other characters, especially Madeline, who looks at herself nude before the bathroom mirror and exclaims that she can't waste her body on Moses.) Motives are duplicities: "All higher or moral tendencies lie under suspicion of being rackets." Thus Valentine resembles, ironically, a "judge in Israel, a king." Madeline dresses for the occasion. It is appropriate that Herzog exclaims at one point: "God's veil over things makes them all riddles." And even when he sees Valentine bathing June—a true vision of their relationship—he thinks in terms of "reflection": "As soon as Herzog saw the actual person giving an actual bath, the reality of it, the tenderness of such a buffoon to a little child, his intended violence turned into *theatre*, into something ludicrous." He recognizes his own unreal motives; he sees his role clearly as an "actor." He decides not to carry on the performance. Because he shifts his vision constantly, he is blurred at times to himself and the others—an "apparition" of sorts. But when he returns to his Ludeyville house, the images decrease; there are fewer references to theatre, duplicity, or "faulty" vision. Instead we have the solid object—the piano, the day lilies, and the wine bottles—as if Herzog too assumes real solidity as he flees from his "prison of perception."

The same pattern is evident in one final image. The novel moves from the deformed to the well-formed, the diseased to the healthy. At first Herzog is obsessed by the notion of sickness; he even does his best to be sick. He goes to have a medical checkup when the season "troubles many people, the new roses, even in shop windows, reminding them of their own failures, of sterility and death." He is pronounced healthy, but he cannot completely believe the physician. He continues to think (and remember) in terms of disease: Valentine's wooden leg; the possibility of Wanda's venereal disease; the "genetic effects of radioactivity"; the "disfigured breast" of Sandor Himmelstein; the "body itself, with its two arms and vertical length" as compared to the cross; the "subjective monstrosity" of people which often matches their physical features; and the wasting away of his mother and the death of his father. Gradually he decides to battle such disease —like Henderson who breathes the chill air of New-foundland at the end of his adventures. Again the Ludeyville house is significant. As Herzog gets it into shape—cleaning and painting it with help of Mr. and Mrs. Tuttle—he is symbolically healing himself; he becomes less "dilapidated"—if that is the word—and he stands against all kinds of disfiguring storms. He chooses—or is chosen?—not "to enact the peculiarities of life." *He breathes deeply at home.*

Herzog gives us the opposition of styles we have learned to expect. On the primary level there is the conflict between preaching and prophecy. Herzog preaches to himself, the "reality-instructors" (when they give him a chance), and the dead about truth, wisdom, and justice; but he does not bore us as do Henderson and Dahfu and Augie March. His preaching is turned into prophecy not only by the images I have mentioned (he thinks or remembers in images) but by his letters. These are written to Nietzsche, the Lord, Eisenhower, Ramona, *et al.* on a variety of topics, but they all share similar characteristics—*they seize him unexpectedly; they are living presences; they embody his deepest longings.*

Bellow uses the letters to suggest Herzog's "rage for order." In the introductory chapter they begin as aphorisms: *"No person, no death"; "Grief, Sir, is a species of idleness."* Then they start to gain control; they get longer as they are written to Daisy, his first wife, Ramona, and Wanda. And in the next and succeeding chapters they merge so with his present sensations (text becomes context!) that it is difficult to call them letters any more. *They live in his mind.* One paragraph may fuse the letter and his consciousness to such an extent that the flow of meaning becomes somewhat obscure. The important thing, however, is that as the prophetic letters (some are actually Utopian!) take hold of Herzog, he submits so strongly to them that he looks at himself purely in letter-writing terms. His madness begins to lie in his constant need to write. Thus as he becomes healthier, he turns—or is turned—to the written word less and less. The last chapter contains some extremely long letters to suggest that they are the last word before complete silence. In the Ludeyville house Herzog thinks: "Perhaps he'd stop writing letters. Yes, that was what was coming, in fact. The knowledge that he was done with these letters." And the novel ends with "not a single word." Why? Herzog has reached the point at which prophecy consists in destroying the word so that reality can *be*—without any comment. Not only does preaching become prophecy; prophecy itself becomes vital silence.

Once we understand the basic tension between prophecy and preaching in the novel, we can notice how it transforms the other styles. Because Herzog thinks constantly of "words" for himself and others, we don't get pure realism. He waits for the Grand Central train; he sees what he must see. His consciousness almost fuses with the external world:

> On the sultry platform of Grand Central he opened the bulky *Times* with its cut shreds at the edges, having set the valise at his feet. The hushed electric trucks were rushing by with mail bags, and he stared at the news with a peculiar effort. It was a hostile broth of black print *Moonraceberlin-Khrushehwarncommittee-galacticXrayPhouma*. He saw twenty paces away the white soft face and independent look of a woman in a shining black straw hat which held her head in depth and eyes that even in the signal-dotted obscurity reached him with a force she could never be aware of.

The words "peculiar effort," "hostile," and "force" reflect his preoccupation with the external world as threatening power. So does the interpretation of the woman as "independent"—we wonder whether she is really as strong as he describes her, or whether she is simply a "double" of Madeline for him. The movement of print mirrors his rushing, unstable thoughts as well as electric "reality" itself.

It is a short leap from such realism—I have discussed only one third-person passage; the first-person passages are even more to the point—to fantasy in the novel. The fantasies are generally nightmarish; they engulf Herzog when "reality" and consciousness merge so completely that, as he thinks, "my fantasy spills soup and gravy on everybody, and I want to scream out or faint away." Reality overflows with potential and actual madness. Madeline buys recklessly: "For a week or two, Field's delivery truck was bringing jewelry, cigarette boxes, coats and dresses, lamps, carpets, almost daily. Madeline could not recall making these purchases. In ten days she ran up a twelve-hundred-dollar bill." They make love in a bed full of "big, dusty volumes of an ancient Russian encyclopedia." The courtroom—symbolic of "official truth"?—becomes especially unreal as the defendants disclose the sordid, mad desires which possess them and make them act in irrational ways; their grotesque stories make Herzog feel "stifled, as if the valves of his heart were not closing and the blood were going back into his lungs." He *sees* the child-murder; it blots out the other "common" sights: "The child screamed, clung, but with both arms the girl hurled it against the wall. On her legs was ruddy hair. And her lover, too, with long jaws and zooty sideburns, watching on the bed. Lying down to copulate, and standing up to kill. Some kill, then cry. Others, not even that." He then rushes into the fantasy of murdering Valentine and Madeline. Perhaps the incident which most affects Herzog is the love of Asphalter, his friend, for a tubercular monkey. He sees in this dream-like relationship his own secret longings for sickness and death: *"True things in grotesque form*, he was thinking." And he must fight, by means of talking out Asphalter's obsessions, his evil allegiances—he realizes that the only thing which saves him (and everyone else) from sinking into private nightmares is "our employment by other human beings and their employment by us. Without this true employment you never dread death, you cultivate it. And consciousness when it doesn't clearly understand what to live for, what to die for, can only abuse and ridicule itself." Thus he relinquishes sick fantasy for true vision, which he finds in comedy and pastoral. These two styles ("modes of perception") finally liberate him.

Herzog constantly changes. We cannot place the hero in one category: he rises above "simple" madness or down-to-earth wisdom; he refuses to submit to our "ideal constructions." Does Herzog act in the present because of his childhood? Is there a "continuity" in life itself? Such questions challenge us as the perspectives change. At times we see Bellow examining Herzog, at other times Herzog examining Herzog. Perhaps the only stability in the entire procedure lies in his (and our) ironic awareness of dualities.

The ironies emerge at first in aphorisms: "*Not that long disease, my life, but that long convalescence, my life.* Herzog maintains that we are "recovering" by various cures or hopes from some original sickness; he is thinking primarily of his recent illness—marriage to Madeline—but by viewing it as "universal" he manages to hold it in comic perspective. He is cured by irony—even when he calls himself a "suffering joker." So intent upon irony is he that he continually plays with words. Most of these word-games—"*O Lord!* . . . *forgive all these trespasses. Lead me not into Penn Station.*"—help him to find complex meaning in the mad situations in which he finds himself. As the novel progresses, these aphorisms, puns, and word-games become the foundation for a profoundly ironic view of humanity. When Herzog and Sono, his Japanese girl friend share a bath, he thinks: "The Jews were strange to the world for a great length of time, and now the

world is being strange to them in return." The events
which occur are put into double perspective here—
Herzog watches himself as Herzog and wandering Jew,
and he finds humor in the "strangeness" in the same
way he finds humor in "Penn Station" and "Tempta-
tion." He creates syntheses (or synthetically), thereby
making a "better" world than the daily one. Perhaps
this is why he somewhat admires the homosexual in
the courtroom who seems to overplay his role and thus
make it new: "He seemed to be giving the world
comedy for comedy, joke for joke. . . . With his bad
fantasy he defied a bad reality. . . ." *Irony defies the
world; it creates a transcendent one in which sickness
and madness are viewed in healthy perspective.* I take
it this is what Herzog has in mind when he proclaims
to Asphalter that there is "something funny about the
human condition, and civilized intelligence makes fun
of its own ideas."

Although irony as a "style of life" dominates Herzog, it apparently disappears when he looks at Nature.
He does not have to be ironic toward "pastoral"—he
delights, as do all of Bellow's urban heroes, in fresh air
and sunlight. On the very first page we find this passage: "When he opened his eyes in the night, the stars
were near like spiritual bodies. Fires, of course; gases—
minerals, heat, atoms, but eloquent at five in the
morning to a man lying in a hammock, wrapped in his
overcoat." Note the words "spiritual" and "eloquent"
—Nature speaks of higher things than divorce or illness; it cannot manipulate us as do the reality-instructors; and it embodies spiritual truths. Often "pastoral"
is juxtaposed to harsh "realism" in the novel. When
Madeline informs Herzog that they "can't live together any more," he sees the sunlight catching an
"ornamental collection" of bottles and "the waves,
the threads of color, the spectral intersecting bars, and
especially a great blot of flaming white on the center
of the wall above Madeline." This vision of patterned
light resembles Henderson's worship of colored light;

it also suggests a better, cleaner world than "marriage." This is not to imply that Herzog views pastoral as completely pure. At the end of his adventures, he accepts rodents and "scrappy lawns"—dark or "unfinished" aspects of Nature. He is "down to earth" in his new-found happiness: "*Something produces intensity, a holy feeling, as oranges produce orange, as grass green, as birds heat.*"

From madness to pastoral; from claustrophobia to violent movement; from *moha* to family feeling—*Herzog* employs the characteristic styles, images, and themes of Bellow's fiction so that it becomes at once private and universal.

7

Conclusion

Bellow's novels are influenced by European and American writers, but they stand alone as fascinating works of art. They aren't locked in one room in the "house of fiction."

Although tensions recur in all of Bellow's novels, they are shaped differently. *Dangling Man* is a journal; *The Victim* is a frantic, tight narrative; *The Adventures of Augie March* is sprawling, "lighthearted" picaresque; *Seize the Day* is a "blest nouvelle"; *Henderson the Rain King* is a parodic romance; and *Herzog* has faint elements of all these. Which is Bellow's greatest achievement?

Dangling Man is the work of a young writer who hasn't completely found his voice. It contains too many echoes of Kafka and Dostoevsky. Its form is not really successful: although the journal entries seem at first to capture Joseph's isolation, they remain entries—repetitive set pieces. So intent is he upon presenting solemn dullness—for this is Joseph's dangling condition—that Bellow mirrors it in his technique. The entries preach mechanically; they lack that humanity which, ironically enough, is sought by Joseph.

Perhaps there is another reason for the static quality: Bellow is too close to his hero; he has not removed himself enough so that he can see complex factors of personality which compel Joseph to act as he does. Thus the "reticence" at crucial points in the novel. The journal entries help Bellow skip over dramatic conflicts or psychological causes by presenting Joseph as a "theoretical" case. Joseph is the *dangling man— the type*—never driving beyond the limitations of his type. These defects do not harm the value of *Dangling Man* as a *representative document*. It does capture the feelings of men waiting for the draft—for something destructive to happen. It is an existential work concerned—as are Camus' *The Stranger* and Sartre's *Nausea*—with the meaning of identity in the modern world, the nature of good and evil, the possibility of fulfillment.

What is immediately striking about *The Victim* is the *tense humanity* of Asa and Allbee. Although they are the typical (almost allegorical) master and slave, Anti-Semite and Jew, they are fully realized human beings who twitch in unique ways. We know more about their backgrounds than we do about Joseph's. We know them well enough to *care* about their complex fates. Furthermore, Bellow has the insight to see that master and slave exist together in Asa *and* Allbee. Diana Trilling is surely correct in claiming that what emerges from their confrontations is "a beautiful balance of forces."

The Victim is a novel with ideas. But that it is as "philosophical" as *Dangling Man* does not mean that it is barren of images, fantastic comedy, etc. The prison, the voyage—these and other images are under the surface, influencing our response to the *total situation* of victims. If they were lacking, *The Victim* would simply be abstract, not "all too human."

The Adventures of Augie March is, of course, a completely different kind of novel—sprawling, picaresque, lighthearted. The first half of it contains as much social truth as *The Victim*, portraying the poverty, corruption, and insanity of the Chicago scene. Only when Bellow describes "mad" Mexico or Europe do we feel that things are getting out of hand—there are too many riches. The novel is a noble failure. Although I admire the larky style, I find that it is somewhat forced—Augie likes to hear himself talk. He preaches. The style hides the fact that Augie is not as clear as we would like him to be. His passivity is disconcerting; his actions are not explained. Of course, it is easy to applaud such "freedom" of movement, such *brio*, in contemporary fiction, but it is also dangerous. Augie—like Walt Whitman, that other masquerader—is at times simply a *persona*—not a person.

If Bellow flees from the real parents—the institutions—in his explorations of *character*, his art can only be full-bodied when he *does* confront them. He does this in *Seize the Day* (and, less so, in *The Victim*). Tommy Wilhelm—that "fair-haired" hippopotamus —is the most interesting character in Bellow's fiction because we see his personal, not "typical," predicament—we see him versus his fathers. He is not sacrificed to craftsmanship, as we feel Asa is to tightness of plot. He is so human that we have ambivalent reactions toward him.

Tensions in character mirror tensions of form. The short novel usually depends less on plot than a lyrical exploration of character—as in Carson McCullers' *The Ballad of the Sad Café*. *Seize the Day* is lyrical at the same time that it is suspenseful—the stock exchange is a mysterious "being" capable of rising or falling; it is chance-ridden. Tommy's emotions are presented in relation to this chance-deity. The unities of plot, time, and place constrain these tensions, making them even more intense. Thus *Seize the Day* achieves a "balance"—intension and extension—only achieved, and much more "schematically," by *The Victim*. It asserts by its complete success that Bellow's art is most powerful when it masters oppositions, ambivalences. *Augie March* is, finally, a joke—a flight from such confrontations. *Seize the Day* is one of the great short novels written by an American—a classic in its own time.

Bellow is trying in *Henderson the Rain King* to confront the tensions of *Seize the Day* on a mythic scale. Henderson is a more interesting character than Augie—although he loves to talk as much as that rogue, he is ultimately more serious and humble. When he has visions, we see them; when he cries, we do. Henderson is, in effect, as full-bodied as Tommy Wilhelm—his style doesn't obscure *character*.

The controlling imagination in *Henderson the Rain King* is vivid. The last fifty pages or so are wonderfully done—the mixture of pathos, comedy, and suspense represents the best of contemporary fiction. It is, unfortunate, that imagination is sacrificed to many conversations in the *middle* of the novel: Bellow still hasn't conquered his preaching; preaching takes the place of plot suspense. The novel is, then, a fascinating grab-bag—jumbled as it is, it is finally a noble failure, perhaps like Melville's *Pierre*.

Herzog is, as I have suggested, a culmination of Bellow's characteristic themes, images, and styles. It is his most complete, substantial novel, especially when it draws upon early experiences which were avoided, or hidden previously. But at times it is highly conscious; there is a quality of sham, theatricality, or self-consciousness which rises to the surface and undercuts our complete sympathy. Thus it lacks the utter humanity of *Seize the Day*.

Although *Seize the Day* is Bellow's greatest achievement, *Herzog* and *The Victim* are almost as good (especially *The Victim*). Of course, these and the ones I think are unsuccessful—*Dangling Man*, *The Adventures of Augie March*, and *Henderson*—are probably the best American post-war novels. It is too early to "place" Bellow, but we can see even now that he has produced a significant body of work—mature, human, imaginative—which will be read fifty years from now. Can we say this of many living writers?

Notes

I have noted references to only Bellow's nonfiction and to secondary sources.

1 — The First Story

1. The "fat gods" phrase is taken from Bellow's tribute to Isaac Rosenfeld, *Partisan Review*, 23 (Fall, 1956), 567.

2 — The Themes

1. Saul Bellow, "The Sealed Treasure," *The Writer's Dilemma* (London: Oxford University Press, 1961), p. 60. This essay first appeared in *Times Literary Supplement* of July 1, 1960, 414, as part of the "Limits of Control" series.

2. Saul Bellow, "On Isaac Rosenfeld," 567.

3. *Ibid*.

4. "Pig Heaven," Bellow's phrase, appears in "The Sealed Treasure," p. 60.

5. *Ibid*., p. 67.   6. *Ibid*.

7. Erich Fromm, *Escape from Freedom* (New York: Rinehart, 1941), p. 251.

8. *Ibid*.

9. "A Discipline of Nobility: Saul Bellow's Fiction," *Kenyon Review*, 24 (Spring, 1962), 209. Mr. Klein's comments are especially helpful.

10. *Ibid*.   11. *Ibid*., 207.

12. Cf. "Filthy Lucre," *Life Against Death* (Middletown: Wesleyan University Press, 1959), pp. 234–304.

13. Bellow, "On Isaac Rosenfeld," 567.

14. Brown, "Filthy Lucre," p. 236.

15. Saul Bellow, "A Spanish Letter," *Partisan Review*, 15 (February, 1948), 222-23.

16. Saul Bellow, "The Uses of Adversity," *The Reporter*, 21 (October 1, 1959), 45.

17. For an interesting discussion of money in *Seize the Day* see Edward Schwartz, "Chronicles of the City," *New Republic*, 135 (December 3, 1956), pp. 20-21.

18. Bellow, "The Sealed Treasure," p. 67.

19. Saul Bellow, "Distractions of Fiction Writer," *The Living Novel*, ed. Granville Hicks (New York: Macmillan, 1957), p. 6. The essay contains Bellow's important statements about his craft.

20. Saul Bellow, "Hemingway and The Image of Man," *Partisan Review*, 20 (May–June, 1953), 342. Bellow's remarks here should be compared with those of Joseph against modern "hardboiled" attitudes.

21. *Ibid.*, 338.

22. Fromm, *Escape From Freedom*, p. 241.

23. *Ibid.* Other interesting studies of conformity in contemporary America are *The Lonely Crowd, The Organization Man,* and *Life in the Crystal Palace.*

24. Bellow, "Distractions of a Fiction Writer," p. 13.

25. Saul Bellow, "The French as Dostoevsky Saw Them," *New Republic*, 132 (May 23, 1955), pp. 17-20. As will be obvious from my later discussion, Dostoevsky is a major influence, giving Bellow the "underground man" as well as the "plot" of *The Victim.*

26. Bellow, "Hemingway and the Image of Man," 339.

27. Herbert Gold, "Review of *Henderson the Rain King,*" *Nation*, 188 (February 21, 1959), 169.

28. Cf. Dan Jacobson, "The Solitariness of Saul Bellow," *Spectator*, May 22, 1959, 735.

29. *Ibid.*

30. Edmund Bergler, "Writers of Half-Talent," *American Imago*, 14 (Summer, 1957), 155.

31. *Ibid.*, p. 156.

32. Leslie Fiedler, "Saul Bellow," *Prairie Schooner*, 31 (Summer, 1957), 109.

33. Morse Peckham, *Beyond the Tragic Vision* (New York: Braziller, 1962), pp. 42-43.

34. *Ibid.*

35. Cf. his review in *New York Times Book Review*, September 20, 1953, p. 1.

36. Robert Penn Warren, "Man with no Commitments," *New Republic*, 129 (November 2, 1953), p. 23.

37. Chester Eisinger, "Saul Bellow: Love and Identity," *Accent*, 18 (Summer, 1958), 193.

38. Bergler, "Writers of Half-Talent," 155.

39. Bellow, "The Sealed Treasure," p. 63.

40. D. J. Hughes, "Reality and the Hero: *Lolita* and *Henderson the Rain King*," *Modern Fiction Studies*, 6 (Winter, 1960–61), 361.

41. Saul Bellow, "Literary Notes on Khrushchev," *Esquire*, March, 1961, p. 107.

42. *Ibid.*, p. 106.   43. *Ibid.*   44. *Ibid.*

45. Saul Bellow, "Pleasures and Pains of Playgoing," *Partisan Review*, 21 (May–June, 1954), 312.

46. Cf. his book on modern drama, *Lies Like Truth*.

47. Saul Bellow, "Facts that Put Fancy to Flight," *New York Times Book Review*, February 11, 1962, pp. 1, 28.

48. *Ibid.*, p. 1.

49. Cf. Saul Bellow, "A Talk with the Yellow Kid," *The Reporter*, 15 (September 6, 1956), pp. 41–44.

50. The separation of types of characterization from structural images is evident in much of the criticism available on Bellow's fiction.

51. Beside those in *Seize the Day* see the con-man in "The Mexican General," Two Morning Monologues," and "By the Rock Wall."

52. Cf. his remarks about Boehme in *Life Against Death*, pp. 309–310: "Whatever the Christian churches do with him Boehme's position in the Western tradition of mystic hope of better things is central and assured. Backward he is linked, through Paracelsus and alchemy, to the tradition of Christian gnosticism and Jewish cabalism; forward he is linked, through his influence on the romantics Blake, Novalis, and Hegel, with Freud."

53. Wilhelm Reich, *Selected Writings: An Introduction to Orgonomy* (New York: Noonday Press, 1961), p. 146.

54. *Ibid.*, p. 151. Cf. the definition of "neurotic character" as given in the glossary: "The character which, due to chronic bioenergetic stasis, operates according to the principle of compulsive moral regulation" (p. 10).

55. Fiedler, "Saul Bellow," 104.

56. Leslie Fiedler, *The Jew in the American Novel* (New York: Herzl Institute Pamphlet 10, 1959), pp. 61–62.

57. *Ibid.*, p. 61.

58. Maxwell Geismar, "Saul Bellow: Novelist of the Intellectuals," *American Moderns: From Rebellion to Conformity* (New York: Hill and Wang, 1958), p. 223.

59. Theodore J. Ross, "Notes on Saul Bellow," *Chicago Jewish Forum*, 18, p. 24. Although I agree with Mr. Ross, I have argued in *Jews and Americans* (Carbondale: Southern Illinois University Press, 1965) that Bellow and other contemporary American-Jewish writers tend to offer modern equivalents of traditional themes—often they appear to be more rebellious than they really are.

60. Charles I. Glicksberg, "The Theme of Alienation in The American Jewish Novel," *Reconstructionist*, 23 (November 29, 1957), p. 10.

61. Saul Bellow, "Rabbi's Boy in Edinburgh," *Saturday Review*, 39 (March 24, 1956), p. 19.

62. Saul Bellow, "The Swamp of Prosperity," *Commentary*, 28 (July, 1959), 77–9.

63. Saul Bellow. "Laughter in the Ghetto," *Saturday Review*, 36 (May 30, 1953), p. 15.

64. *Ibid.*   65. *Ibid.*

66. Cf. Harold Rosenberg's comments in "The Comedy of the Divine," *The Tradition of the New* (New York: Horizon, 1959). Mr. Rosenberg discusses Mann's Joseph novels as "divine comedy"—Joseph, by being an individual and a character in the God-story, is two-sided, self and not-self—a cosmic joke. Bellow makes the same points about Jewish "doubleness" in his introduction to *Great Jewish Short Stories* (New York: Dell, 1965).

67. Cf. his introduction to Kafka's *The Castle* (New York: Alfred A. Knopf). Kafka, by the way, assumes a crucial position for contemporary Jewish-American writers, especially Isaac Rosenfeld in his short stories ("King Solomon"), Leslie Fiedler, and Bellow himself. Joseph in *Dangling Man* has the same first name as the hero of Kafka's *The Trial*. I have noted Kafka's influence in my *Jews and Americans*.

68. Geismar, "Saul Bellow: Novelist of the Intellecuals," p. 216.

69. Jean-Paul Sartre, *Anti-Semite and Jew* (New York: Evergreen Books, 1960), p. 67.

70. This tale is found in *A Treasury of Yiddish Stories*, ed. Irving Howe and Elizer Greenberg (New York: Meridian, 1959), pp. 626–27.

71. Cf. "Introduction" to the *Treasury*, p. 38.

72. *Ibid.*   73. *Ibid.*, p. 41.

74. *Ibid.*, pp. 40–41.   75. *Ibid.*, p. 38.

76. *Ibid.*

77. Cf. Fiedler, *The Jew in the American Novel*, p. 61.

78. Theodore Solotaroff, "Introduction," *An Age of Enormity* by Isaac Rosenfeld (New York: World, 1962), p. 28. The introduction is particularly important for an understanding of contemporary Jewish-American writing. For other essays on this growing body of literature see Karl Shapiro, "The Jewish Writer in America," *In Defense of Ignorance* (New York: Random House, 1961), pp. 205–217; Theodore Solotaroff. "Philip Roth and *The Jewish Moralists*," Chicago Review, Winter, 1959, 87–99; Alfred Kazin's autobiography, *A Walker in the City* (New York: Harcourt Brace, 1951); Leslie Fiedler's autobiographical essays in *An End to Innocence* (Boston: Beacon, 1955) and *No! in Thunder* (Boston: Beacon, 1960); and my own *Jews and Americans*.

3 — The Characters

1. Cf., for example, Herbert Gold, "The Heart of the Artichoke," Delmore Schwartz, *The World is a Wedding*; and Sam Astrachan, *An End to Dying*. See my discussion in *Jews and Americans*.

2. This is especially evident in *The World is a Wedding*.

3. "Saul Bellow: Novelist of the Intellectuals," p. 220.

4. "Saul Bellow," 108.

5. But on this matter see Otto Fenichel, *The Psychoanalytic Theory of Neurosis* (New York: W. W. Norton, 1945), p. 334.

6. "The Adventures of Saul Bellow," *Commentary*, (April, 1959), 330.

7. For some interesting comments on the subject of Bellow's children see Ralph Freedman, "Saul Bellow:

The Illusion of Environment," *Wisconsin Studies in Contemporary Literature*, I (Winter, 1960), 50–65.

8. Erickson's *Young Man Luther* is a very effective study of "life choices" made in adolescence.

9. Bellow, "The Sealed Treasure," p. 64.

4—The Images

1. Marcus Klein in "A Discipline of Nobility" mentions imagery of weight in general terms, but he does not look closely at the *texture* of each novel.

2. As I indicate at the end of this chapter, Bellow's images are archetypal—weight is related to the cross Christ bears.

3. Cf. Klein's essay for valuable comments on "stylistic weight": "And if all history and culture are rejected in a style that borrows widely from the world's accumulation of literature, that fact is more than irony. Bellow's style which beginning with *Augie March* has become a racy vehicle bearing great freights of knowledge, is a thing that simultaneously admits and dismisses clutter," (210–211).

4. Thomas Mann, "Dostoevsky—in Moderation," Preface to *The Short Novels of Dostoevsky* (New York: Dial Press, 1945), p. XIV.

5. This "sermon" is important for suggesting new directions in Bellow's images and themes. But it is a wonderful achievement in itself. Herbert Gold chooses it for inclusion in his anthology, *Fiction of the Fifties* (New York: Doubleday, 1959).

6. Rosenfeld, *The Age of Enormity*, pp. 183–84.

7. *Ibid.*, p. 184.

8. Klein, "A Discipline of Nobility," 221. Although Mr. Klein views the animal nature of Bellow's heroes in general terms, he neglects many specific images in each of the novels.

9. D. J. Hughes "Reality and the Hero: *Lolita* and *Henderson the Rain King*," *Modern Fiction Studies*, 6 (Winter 1960–1961), 358.

10. *Ibid.*, 359.

11. In *Twentieth Century Authors*: First Supplement, ed. Stanley J. Kunitz (New York, 1955), p. 73.

12. Ralph Freedman, "Saul Bellow: The Illusion of

Environment," *Wisconsin Studies in Contemporary Literature*, 1 (Winter, 1960), 52–53.

13. *New York Times Book Review*, February 15, 1959, pp. 1, 34.

14. *Ibid.*, p. 1.   15. *Ibid.*

16. Anthony West, *The New Yorker*, 29 (September 26, 1953), p. 142.

17. *Ibid.*, p. 140.

18. Saul Bellow, "Facts that Put Fancy to Flight," p. 28.

19. *Ibid.*

5—The Styles

1. Freedman, "Saul Bellow: The Illusion of Environment," 51.

2. Hughes, "Reality and the Hero," 348–49.

3. In *A Treasury of Yiddish Stories*, ed. Irving Howe and Elizer Greenberg (New York: World, 1955), p. 611.

4. *Ibid.*   5. *Ibid.*, p. 612.

6. I am using the Constance Garnett translation.

7. Saul Bellow, "Literary Notes on Khruschev," p. 106.

8. Hughes, "Reality and the Hero," 361.

9. J. Huizinga, *Homo Ludens* (Boston: Beacon, 1955), pp. 3–4.

10. Klein, "A Discipline of Mobility," 212.

11. E. M. Forster, *Aspects of the Novel* (New York: Harvest Books, 1954), p. 125.

12. *Ibid.*, pp. 125–26.   13. *Ibid.*, p. 126.   14. *Ibid.*, pp. 132–33.

15. Bellow, "Hemingway and the Image of Man," 338.

16. *Ibid.*, 342.

17. Saul Bellow, "Dreiser and the Triumph of Art," *Commentary*, 11 (May, 1951), 503.

18. *Ibid.*, 502.

19. Bellow, "Distractions of a Fiction Writer," p. 6.

20. Bellow, "The Sealed Treasure," p. 67.

21. *Ibid.*, p. 65.

Index